THE SOVIET CONTROL STRUCTURE: Capabilities for Wartime Survival

(

THE SOVIET CONTROL STRUCTURE:
Capabilities for Wartime Survival

Harriet Fast Scott
and William F. Scott

Crane Russak · New York
National Strategy Information Center, Inc.

The Soviet Control Structure:
Capabilities for Wartime Survival

Published in the United States by

Crane, Russak & Company, Inc.
3 East 44th Street
New York, NY 10017

Copyright © 1983 National Strategy Information Center, Inc.
111 East 58th Street
New York, NY 10022

Library of Congress Cataloging in Publication Data

Scott, William Fontaine, 1919-
The Soviet control structure.

(Strategy papers; no. 39)
1. Command and control systems.   2. Soviet Union—Politics
and government—1953-   .   3. Atomic warfare—Safety
measures.   4. Soviet Union—Civil defense.   5. Civil
supremacy over the military—Soviet Union.
I. Scott, Harriet Fast.   II. Title.   III. Series: Strategy papers
(National Strategy Information Center); no. 39
UB212.S36 1983   355.3′0947   83-2004
ISBN 0-8448-1452-0 (pbk.)

Printed in the United States of America

Table of Contents

PREFACE

Wars begin in men's minds, as the UNESCO charter says, and all nations think about war. In time of peace, some think offensively, of surprise strikes and quick victory. Others think defensively, of deterring, bargaining, or cajoling the would-be aggressor away from his sinister dreams.

Not too long ago, it was easy to tell the difference between the two. The Nazis and Fascists gloried openly in conquest by arms. Their targeted victims in the free world dithered and tried desperately to see no evil, believing that nothing was worse than one more war. No one could, or did, mistake Neville Chamberlain for Adolf Hitler.

In our time, that distinction no longer holds. Everyone asserts an abhorrence of war. Everyone is for peace. And everyone is a victim, threatened by someone else and compelled to take up arms in self-defense. If anyone now takes over the world, it will be through fending off some mortal threat and only trying to make the world safe for him to live in.

According to one substantial chunk of conventional wisdom in the free countries, these X-equals-Y propositions are the proper starting point for the war-and-peace agenda. Critics like Paul Warnke contend that the superpowers are "apes on a treadmill," goading each other mindlessly toward calamity. Others extend the equation to areas like the Caribbean, where American devotion to "military solutions" is counterpart to Soviet devotion to the same thing, and to other continents where Soviet imperialism is matched by U.S. imperialism.

The merits or demerits of this mind-set apart for a moment, the effect on the free nations is disabling. Since the Soviet managers do not have to cope with similar accusations from their own subjects, they have a ready-made psychological warfare weapon against their free-world adversaries. When General Secretary Andropov assures the ten year-old child in Maine that he solemnly abjures "first use" of nuclear arms, many in this and other non-Communist countries nod in approval. When President Reagan points out the huge advantages in key weapons systems that the Soviets would "freeze," he is scoffed at and urged to be more "flexible." You must make the first disavowal, he is told, the first spiking of the bombs.

How, then, is the thoughtful layperson to come to grips with the truth? Is there a truth that isn't being told? Is the "plague-on-both-your-houses" his only recourse? Or, is there some measure of the real differences between this country and the Soviet Union?

Yes, there is. It is to tour the sociology of Soviet totalitarianism with the authors of this volume. Harriet Fast Scott and William F. Scott are longtime students of Soviet ruling techniques, particularly in the field of war-planning and war-making. And, any reader of this work who follows them with an open mind must come out disabused of any notion that the Soviet rulers are just a lot of administrators trying to live and let live.

What the Scotts have put together is a canvas of a Soviet society mobilized — in the fullest sense of the word — for peace and war, with the dividing line between them all but obliterated. In Clausewitz's phrase, war is not even "politics by other means," but politics under another label. Not even Hitler could match the thoroughness with which the USSR is poised to wage — and win — the next war.

Mobilization plans are total; nothing is left to chance. Soviet forces, for example, are not to be left unprotected against the elements in a campaign that went awry. Every institution of the society has its role in that conflict: Party structure, government, *Komsomol,* a grass-roots Professional Union, "volunteer" societies, even local service establishments such as firefighting and construction. The High Command is in place. Doctrine, strategy, logistics, technology, forces blend completely. The industrial assembly lines are concentrated even now to turning out what will be needed in the conflict.

Command and control structures are ready to function. Civil defense covers every category of leader down to the peasant. Casualties are accounted for. The population, young and old, is psychologically indoctrinated for whatever may be demanded of them. And, climaxing the long train of preparations for combat are those for the aftermath, when the victorious survivors reconstruct their country. What have the free nations to compare?

All this does not make the Soviets ten feet tall. Their planning can claim no tribute from their economic performance. In fact, over-planning has been in many instances the bane of their existence, and that may yet betray them in a war. And, as the Scotts remind us, their captive "allies" and their own minorities are vulnerabilities that all their planning cannot eliminate.

The sobering thing, however, is the deliberation with which they go about their planning. It is all routine, institutionalized. War, including nuclear war, is not "unthinkable." True or not, they think they can wage nuclear war and win it, and behave accordingly. It is to them all a matter of how, when and where, not whether, as their target adversaries agonize over so deeply.

The price for this Soviet self-assurance, as the Scotts make clear, is enormous. Not only are material resources committed in massive amounts to the effort, but so are the sacrifices in human life. It is often asserted by apologists in the Western democracies that the millions of Soviet citizens who died in World War II have left a trauma about any future war. That may be true of the ordinary Soviet people, but their leaders seem very willing to repeat that history and equally confident that they can impose comparable sacrifices on their subjects again. The lesson of the Great Patriotic War, as they seemed to have learned it, is that Soviet resiliency and resolve will again prevail.

Here is the bottom line of the clash of their society with ours. For very commendable reasons, we cannot call for the same level of sacrifice. In peacetime, the Soviet managers can make their people acquiesce in arms spending — much of it for adventures far from their borders — twice or more what the American people will tolerate. The loss of life that drove the United States out of Vietnam is building toward comparable dimensions in Afghanistan, yet the Soviet High Command is redoubling its efforts there, not considering getting out.

Why this is so is beyond the scope of this volume and this discussion. The democracies, and Americans in particular, have given much thought in recent years to what is called "national will," uneasy with the evidence that it has eroded markedly. Whatever national will is composed of — morale, confidence in leaders and policy, belief in the righteousness of one's cause — the touchstone is the willingness to back up thought with act. The ability of totalitarian regimes to spend lives and treasures more freely than democracies can even contemplate is not regarded as a virtue in our world—and rightly so. But it is a fact of life that in present circumstances will be ignored or fudged by wishful thinking at peril to our survival.

Part of the tragedy of World War II was the failure of the potential victims to study Hitlerian Germany's sociology early enough and seriously enough. That excuse—if, indeed it is an excuse—will not avail again, thanks to the work of scholars like the Scotts.

Gerald L. Steibel
Vice President and Director of Studies
National Strategy Information Center, Inc.

June 1983

1
Introduction

A Legacy for Control

A controlled society requires a control structure. The Communist Party of the Soviet Union (CPSU) maintains its power through a system of controls, which has been improved continuously over the past six decades. This system has stood the test of the Civil War, the collectivization of agriculture, the purges of the 1930s, and World War II. During the first 60 years of the Soviet state more Soviet people died at the hands of their fellow countrymen than in war with external enemies. Throughout this period, the Party's control has never seriously been challenged. In the United States a million deaths might seem unacceptable in a war; Stalin brought about the deaths of 20 times that number to consolidate his own power.

The men who run the Soviet state today lived through the purges, the mass starvation, and World War II. They have used the system initiated by Lenin, exploited by Stalin, and perfected by the present Kremlin leaders to maintain and improve their own power positions as well as to retain control of the populace in peace and in war.

In the event of a nuclear war, a nation's leadership must be able to maintain effective control over the people and the economy. Such control is crucial — it could mean a nation's survival. Even in a limited nuclear exchange the capability of the leadership to direct all elements of a nation's warfighting structure, economy, and population would remain of paramount importance. How effective would the existing Soviet control structure be should that nation come under nuclear attack?

The current system of controls in the Soviet Union has obvious advantages in a wartime situation. Soviet writers maintain that centralized control was essential to Soviet successes in World War II. Soviet spokesmen today emphasize the continuing need to maintain this high degree of centralization.[1]

1

The necessity for centralized control is rooted in the nature of the Soviet state. Considerable segments of the population in a number of the Soviet republics are composed of many nationalities; they may have little loyalty to the Communist Party and an actual dislike of the Russians as a nationality. In the initial days of the German invasion of 1941, before Hitler's true intentions were realized, many people in Soviet villages and towns welcomed the Germans as liberators. Even in peacetime the Kremlin leadership depends upon internal military forces to carry out its edicts.

Loss of control by the leadership or any significant diminution of Soviet military capability could result in acute instability, both internally and around Soviet borders. With the probable exception of Bulgaria, the neighbors of the Soviet Union, from Finland to China, are either actually or potentially hostile to Soviet influence or domination. This antipathy applies equally to the Warsaw Pact nations of Eastern Europe.

More than any other government on earth, the Soviet leadership is preoccupied with military affairs. The Party's basic military policy, officially expressed as the military doctrine of the state, is that "the armed forces, the population, the whole Soviet nation, must be prepared for the eventuality of nuclear rocket war."[2]

Soviet rulers over the years have developed a system for ensuring control of the population in the event of war or in any situation that might threaten the established order. A knowledge of this system is essential for those seeking to understand the strengths and weaknesses of the Soviet state.

This analysis will attempt to provide a better understanding of the complex organizational system for control that has evolved in the Soviet Union, and will devote primary attention to those bodies most responsible for directing and continuing a modern war effort. These include the current Council of Defense, the Main Military Council, and the General Staff. The study will cover the probable transformation of the first two bodies during a period of high tension, or after initiation of war, into something similar to the State Committee of Defense (GKO) and the Headquarters of the supreme High Command (The *Stavka* of the VGK), which operated during World War II.

The Communist Party of the Soviet Union operates a unique control structure, maintaining an internal (Party) control infrastructure as well as exercising control through all other major Soviet agencies, from the Ministry of Defense to the various civilian ministries. The Party is assisted by the *Komsomol* (Young Communist League), which provides additional support for various organizations and activities. The apparatus of the Soviet government is another structure. The Party, the *Komsomol,* and government organizations down to the regional level will be described in this report, with emphasis placed on their relationships with the Armed Forces.

Soviet military districts and theaters of military operations (TVDs) are critical elements in ensuring control of the population in a nuclear war situation. The relationship of these districts to Party control authorities provides a means for all edicts issued by a central Party control structure to be carried out. In theory at least, if the central control structure were destroyed, regional Party organizations, in conjunction with commanders of military districts, could still retain a control capability. This analysis includes a description of the organization of the military districts and their role in mobilization, together with the work of the military commissariats.

Soviet civil defense is also covered, to include both its civilian and military components as well as the direction and control provided by the Ministry of Defense. Related to the civil defense structure are several measures, such as "moral-political" preparation of the population and the military indoctrination of Soviet youth. Psychological preparation of the population for the possibility of nuclear war could be an important element in the ability of the Soviet leadership to maintain control, and will be examined in that light.

The Soviet leadership's total control capabilities will be analyzed, based on an examination of the control organs as they exist today and as they would most likely be structured after the onset of hostilities. Attention is also given to the means of directing the economy and the population during a conflict, pending the restoration and reinstitution of a permanent control apparatus.

The Potential for Survival

A brief look at the years during which the present Soviet leadership matured may indicate how well or in what manner the Soviet control structure might be exercised. Several members of the Soviet Politburo of 1983 were in their early, formative years during World War I, the Revolution, and the Civil War. In those years more than 12 million civilians died from famine or military actions.[3] These do not include the 2 million men the Imperial Russian Army lost in World War I.

Between 1926 and 1939 approximately 20 million more Soviet citizens died of starvation caused by Stalin's forced collectivization of agriculture, the deliberately imposed conditions in the forced labor camps, and outright executions. During this time some of the current Politburo leaders were in their thirties.

Livestock losses reflect the condition of the Soviet Union in the 1930s. In 1928 the number of cattle was estimated at 60.1 million; it had decreased to 33.5 million by 1934. By 1953 this number had climbed back to only 56.6 million. The sheep population was reduced from 104 million in 1928 to less than 40 million by 1934. In 1928 the peoples of Central Asia possessed approximately 1.8 million camels, but they had only 277,000 by 1935.[4]

The massive military purges of the 1930s, which were responsible for a higher percentage of deaths among the top Soviet military leaders than the fighting during World War II, were described in the 1960s. According to an official publication of the Soviet Ministry of Defense:

> In 1937-1938, and also subsequent to that time, as a result of unfounded mass repressions, the flower of the command and political staff of the Red Army was killed. As "agents of foreign intelligence" and "enemies of the people," three marshals of the Soviet Union (of five at the time) — M. N. Tukhachevskiy, V. K. Blyukher, A. I. Yegorov were condemned and killed; all of the troop commanders of military districts were killed, including I. P. Uborevich and I. E. Yakir, and also the heads of fleets, V. M. Orlov and M. V. Viktorov; outstanding organizers of party-political work in the army were killed; . . . many outstanding military figures and heroes of the Civil War

were either killed or imprisoned for long periods. . . . All corps commanders and almost all division commanders and brigade commanders were eliminated from the Army, also about half of the regimental commanders, members of military councils and chiefs of political administrations of military districts, the majority of corps, division and brigade military commissars and about one-third of those in regiments. . . .[5]

Marshal D. F. Ustinov, Soviet Minister of Defense and Politburo member since 1976, was 30 years old when the military purges were at their height. He had been graduated from the Leningrad Military-Mechanical Institute in 1934 and was too junior to have been caught up in Stalin's net. But the deaths of so many senior officers may account for his becoming "People's Commissar of Armaments" in 1941 at the age of 33. On November 19, 1944, he was promoted to general–colonel (3 stars)*. The late Marshal L. I. Brezhnev also may have owed his rapid promotion to general officer during World War II to the fact that Stalin had eliminated practically all of the senior political officers in 1937 and 1938.

Soviet secrecy, security, and disinformation were such at that time that leading figures in the West were scarcely aware of Stalin's purges, the mass starvation, and the labor camps that spread across the entire U.S.S.R. (The United States Ambassador in Moscow, Joseph Davies — a successful businessman prior to his appointment — considered the measures taken by Stalin completely justified,[6] and Professor Harold Laski asserted that Andrey Vyshinsky, the Soviet prosecutor, was "a man whose passion was law reform."[7]) The full extent of the purges is still carefully

---

Editor's Note: As is customary in the Soviet Armed Forces, titles of senior Soviet officers are rendered throughout this text as general-major, general-lieutenant, and general-colonel. A one-star general in the Soviet Army is a *general-mayor,* and a two-star general is a *general-leytenant.* Although the English terms lieutenant general, major general, etc., are the linguistic equivalents of these titles, they do not correspond to the actual gradations of military rank in the Soviet hierarchy.

kept from the Soviet people, and Aleksandr Solzhenitsyn's *The Gulag Archipelago*[8] ranks high among the books that Soviet authorities attempt to keep from entering the U.S.S.R.

In June 1941, Hitler invaded the Soviet Union. Despite the purges, the forced labor camps (which still existed), and the millions who had died from starvation primarily as a result of Stalin's actions, the Soviet system still functioned. Although the harsh policies of Hitler did contribute in large measure to a consolidation of efforts by the Soviet people against the invading forces, the ability of the Soviet leadership to maintain effective control over the armed forces, the population, and the economy was remarkable.

Another 20 million Soviet citizens died as a direct or indirect result of the German invasion, and 25 million were made homeless. The war destroyed 1,710 cities and "city-size settlements" as well as 70,000 towns and villages, 32,000 plants and factories, and 65,000 kilometers of railroads. In the countryside 98,000 *kolkhozes* (collective farms), 1,876 *sovkhozes* (state farms), and 2,800 machine-tractor stations were completely ruined. Livestock losses included 7 million horses, 17 million cattle, 20 million hogs, and 27 million sheep.[9]

Even during World II the Soviet forced labor camps were filled with men, women, and often children. In 1944 the Vice President of the United States, Henry Wallace, visited one of the more infamous camp zones in Magadan. Aware of his interest in agriculture, his Soviet hosts took him to a farm in the area, telling him that people who sympathized with the Germans were interned there. Wallace never suspected that the watchtowers had been demolished for his visit, nor that the girl swineherds were from the People's Commissariat of Internal Affairs (NKVD) office staff and not women prisoners.

Purges of various types continued between the end of World War II and 1953, the year of Stalin's death. Millions of Soviet citizens were imprisoned in forced labor camps, where they died by the hundreds of thousands.[10] As before, the Kremlin's rule was never seriously threatened.

At the time of Stalin's death, Marshal Brezhnev was 47 years of age, and Marshal Ustinov was 45. They had participated in one way or another in World War II, as had other members of the current Politburo, and they became leaders in the postwar period. These leaders survived internal struggles in which approximately 30 million of their countrymen died so that the Party could build its power base. Another 20 million died during the "Great Patriotic War." It would be impossible for United States political leaders to seriously consider taking the measures the Soviet leaders have witnessed in order to maintain control of a nation. It would be outside Americans' realm of experience and beyond their comprehension. Nevertheless, the Soviet control system has functioned successfully for over 60 years, during periods of external war and vast internal repression. And, if Soviet writings can be believed at all, this control system has been modified and adjusted to take the possibility of a nuclear war into consideration.

NOTES

1. M. P. Skirdo, *Narod, Armiya, Polkovodets* [The People, the Army, the Commander]. Moscow: Voyenizdat, 1970, p. 147.

2. S. S. Lototskiy, *The Soviet Army.* Moscow: Progress Publishers, 1971, p. 332. For a discussion on how the Soviet Armed Forces, the economy, and the population should be prepared for nuclear war, see V. D. Sokolovskiy, *Soviet Military Strategy,* Third Edition, with analysis and commentary by Harriet Fast Scott. New York: Crane Russak & Company, Inc., 1975, pp. 304–334.

3. See Michael T. Florinsky, Editor, *Encyclopedia of Russia and the Soviet Union.* New York: McGraw-Hill Book Co., 1961, p. 443.

4. Ibid., p. 83.

5. P. N. Pospelov, ed., *Velikaya Otechestvennaya Voyna Sovetskogo Soyuza: Kratkaya Istoriya* [The Great Patriotic War of the Soviet Union: A Short History]. Moscow: Voyenizdat, 1965, pp. 39–40. Since the mid-1960s there has been a continuing attempt in the Soviet Union to glorify Stalin. The Kremlin leaders would never permit statements showing Stalin's crimes to any extent to be published today.

6. Joseph E. Davies, *Mission to Moscow.* New York: Simon & Schuster, 1941, pp. 42–43.

7. Robert Conquest, *The Great Terror.* New York: Macmillan, 1968, p. 506.

8. See Aleksandr Solzhenitsyn, *The Gulag Archipelago.* New York: Harper & Row, Volumes 1, 2, and 3, published in 1973, 1974, and 1976

respectively. These books provide new data on the extent of Stalin's purges and labor camps. Such camps, in reduced numbers, still exist.

9. N. Voznesenskiy, *Voyennaya Ekonomika SSSR v Period Otechestvennoy Voyny* (Military Economy of the U.S.S.R. in the Period of the Patriotic War). Moscow: Politizdat, 1947, p. 159. Voznesenskiy, a member of the Politburo and Chairman of GOSPLAN during the war, apparently revealed more in this book concerning Soviet war losses than Stalin had anticipated. As a result, Voznesenskiy was shot shortly after the book appeared.

10. For an excellent account of this period, see Aleksandr Solzhenitsyn, *The Gulag Archipelago,* Vol. 3.

2
Planning for Wartime Conditions

Facing the Possibility of a Nuclear War

The new Soviet military doctrine, announced by Nikita Khrushchev on January 14, 1960, was reaffirmed and further explained
in the report to the 22nd Party Congress in October 1961. Marshal
R. Ya. Malinovskiy, the Soviet Minister of Defense, told the Congress that a basic tenet of the new doctrine was that "a world war
. . . inevitably will take the form of a nuclear missile war."[1]

The new doctrine required a corresponding strategy. In August
1962, shortly before the Cuban missile confrontation, *Military
Strategy,* edited by Marshal V. D. Sokolovskiy, appeared in Moscow bookstores. Apparently, Sokolovskiy and a group of key Soviet strategists had been given the task of presenting an unclassified
version of the new military strategy to be read by both the general
public and the military. One chapter of this book, entitled "Preparing a Country for the Repulsion of Aggression," described
"the preparation of the population"[2] for nuclear war conditions.
This chapter remained virtually unchanged through all three edi-
tions of the book (1962, 1963, and 1968). It is most instructive to
review today what Marshal Sokolovskiy advocated in 1962 — before the Cuban crisis — to prepare the nation for nuclear war,
and what has been accomplished in the Soviet Union since that
time.

Practically all of the points made in *Military Strategy* concerning survival in nuclear war can be found in other Soviet military
and political writings. As outlined by Sokolovskiy, "a nation must
be prepared for waging war for a protracted period of time," and
for surviving "under massive nuclear strikes of the enemy with
the fewest possible losses." While under attack, "a high moral-

political state of the population must be maintained," and the people must be convinced they will achieve victory.[3]

As for armed forces, the ideal situation would be to maintain at all times sufficient forces-in-being to wage nuclear war. However, the cost of such forces would be "economically impossible for even the strongest country." In time of peace, nevertheless, military forces must be maintained at levels sufficient "to deliver a well-timed nuclear strike, repel a surprise air attack, actively wage military operations on land and at sea, and seize the strategic initiative."[4]

Speedy and effective mobilization must be given primary attention in preparing for the possibility of nuclear war. Cadre formations must already be in specific localities, ready to form units through mobilization of reserve manpower within each local area. If necessary, the peacetime period of universal military training should be shortened in order to "discharge into the reserves" the maximum number of trained people. Since the number of officers transferring each year from active duty to the reserves will be insufficient to meet mobilization requirements, a reserve of young officers is created by awarding commissions to sergeants who, after having completed two years of military duty, are discharged into the reserves. This applies especially to young men with secondary and higher education.[5]

Mobilization will have the greatest impact on Ground Forces and the Troops of Civil Defense. New units will have to be organized and deployed to fill the gaps created by losses brought about by enemy nuclear attacks. Troops must be stationed throughout the country, since every area could be subjected to nuclear destruction. Preparation of the Armed Forces for nuclear war conditions requires coordinated activities of both civilian and military agencies.

Regarding the national economy, any productive capabilities that could satisfy wartime requirements must be created in peacetime. In past wars a nation might have had the opportunity to expand its productive capacity after the outbreak of war; in a nuclear war this expansion will probably be impossible. Standardization between civilian and military goods should be accomplished whenever possible, and equipment parts should be interchangeable. Within the nation production should be organized by economic regions. Each region should be self-sufficient, insofar as possible, and organized for the minimum shipment of supplies from one region to another. Critical industries should be placed underground.[6] When this is impossible, the critical components of the plant should be enclosed in concrete shelters.

Food reserves for the possibility of war must be maintained at all times. Agricultural activities must be organized so that workers of military age can go into the Armed Forces, and food production can be continued by women, children, and those men too old for military service. Equipment used in agricultural work — automobiles, tractors, prime movers, trucks, etc. — should be compatible with those used in the Armed Forces in order that they might serve as a ready reserve for military units.

Careful attention must be given to transport and communications — a critical requirement due to the vast distances between cities in the Soviet Union. Motor transport is less affected by nuclear attack than rail and should be expanded. For transporting fuel and oil, pipelines are more efficient than either rail or motor transport, and less vulnerable to nuclear attack than are railroads.[7] Working communication systems are essential for notification and control of the population in nuclear war conditions. Duplicate facilities should be provided, and peacetime and wartime communications must be constructed on the principle of strict continuity. Key communications centers should be established in underground facilities for maximum protection from nuclear blasts.

The entire population should be given basic military training. They might be required to take actions "against spies and saboteurs" at any time and must be ready for partisan operations. The entire population should understand and be trained in firing rifles and shotguns, and in the operation and use of antitank weapons.

The tasks outlined in *Military Strategy* for "preparing a country for the repulsion of aggression" may be compared to a Soviet five-year economic plan which gives production goals intended by the Party leadership. Some of the goals will be met, others will be reduced, and a few will be quietly dropped. Nevertheless, the five-year plan provides a yardstick against which actual Soviet performance may be measured. In a similar manner, the goals stated by Marshal Sokolovskiy in 1962 concerning preparation of the country for the possibility of nuclear war can now be examined with respect to what has been dropped and what has been achieved. Military training for the entire population has been intensified. In 1971, Marshal A. A. Grechko reported that "the movement of the productive forces to the east, the bringing of them closer to the sources of raw materials and fuel, and the scattered placement of them in the economic regions will significantly raise the defense capability of the Soviet motherland and make our industry less vulnerable in the event that imperialism unleashes a nuclear missile war."[8]

To survive in conditions of nuclear war, it will not be sufficient for leaders just to determine theoretically a nation's needs for preparing to withstand a nuclear attack, and even to carry out some of the requirements. The Soviet leadership will need a way to implement control measures to force the population to continue the war effort or to rebuild the nation according to prepared plans.

Basic Mechanisms for Control

Soviet legislation specifies measures to ensure that control can be maintained throughout the nation in the event of an emergency or critical situation. These measures include a special category of "wartime laws." Other Soviet laws provide for the requisition from the population of whatever goods might be needed by state authorities. These laws are discussed in some detail in Soviet textboooks and various publications.

"Wartime laws" are explained in the *Soviet Military Encyclopedia* as being "legal acts and regulations, the action of which is limited to *time of war.*" As described further:

> . . . Wartime laws might be adopted by legislation before and after the entry (factual or legal) of a state into war, but applying only in the period of the state of war. It may spread to all territory of the state which is in a state of war or only to separate regions, concerning which instructions are given in the very laws of the highest agencies of state power.

Soviet spokesmen attempt to justify laws, and to make them acceptable to the populace, with the following assertions:

> Wartime laws in the U.S.S.R. reflect the will of the Soviet people and are called up to protect their interests in a period of armed defense of the Motherland from attack from outside. These laws are based on general democratic principles and institutions of Soviet law. They can regulate civil, administrative, criminal, criminal-procedure, and other legal relationships. In time of war the removal of property from the owner is permitted with payment of the cost of what has been taken in the interests of the defense of the country (requisition), the carrying out of labor mobilization of the population, the enlisting of citizens for various duties (transportation, for example).[9]

Special attention in the "wartime laws" is given to certain actions which might incur severe penalties.

> Soviet criminal legislation recognizes as criminal actions in time of war evasion of labor mobilization or the non-fulfillment of other obligations, to include the evasion of paying taxes. In comparison to peacetime, more severe penalties are envisaged in time of war. Other criminal actions are evasion of the call for mobilization, or from subsequent calls to military service in the Armed Forces, U.S.S.R., for anti-Soviet agitation and propaganda, for various military crimes (insubordination, disobeying orders, violent actions against commissioned or noncommissioned officers, violation of service regulations, desertion, misuse of powers, etc.). For especially severe military crimes, perpetrated in time of war, the court might use the death sentence. One of the special acts, meant for use in time of war, is the Edict of the Supreme Soviet of the U.S.S.R. dated June 22, 1941, "On Martial Law." According to it the rights of corresponding military commands were broadened: it could hold suspected persons in areas declared under martial law, forbid the entry into these areas and exit from them, issue decrees and so forth, obligatory for all the population.[10]

It is interesting to note that the *Soviet Military Encyclopedia* published in the late 1970s, refers to an Edict of the Supreme Soviet dated June 22, 1941, the day of the German invasion. The Soviet leadership of today is still conditioned by the concept of total war, which many experienced both during the Civil War and the Great Patriotic War, as the Soviets refer to the period from June 1941 to 1945 when they participated in World War II against Hitler.

In the United States the very concept of "requisition" would be beyond the understanding of the majority of citizens. Soviet spokesmen describe it matter-of-factly:

> Requisition: In the U.S.S.R. requisitioning is conducted in exceptional circumstances (natural disasters, epidemics, military conditions), in case of especially serious need, on the basis of laws and edicts of the government of the U.S.S.R. or a union republic. In emergency situations it might be carried out by edict of the local organs of power with subsequent reporting to the government.[11]

The new Constitution of the U.S.S.R., adopted in 1977, states that the Presidium of the Supreme Soviet can "proclaim martial law in particular localities or throughout the country for the defense of the U.S.S.R."[12] Textbooks on military legislation further define the conditions of martial law and describe how it is enforced. Basic provisions are as follows:

> The authority of the military command under conditions of martial law must be examined separately. Martial law is a special state-legal regime, introduced by the Presidium of the Supreme Soviet of the U.S.S.R. in separate areas or in the whole country under extraordinary circumstances and characterized by the introduction into operation of special (extraordinary) measures in the interests of the defense of the U.S.S.R. One of the characteristic features of martial law is broadening the authority of military powers in the sphere of assuring the defense of the state, state security, and maintenance of public order.[13]

Note that martial law may be declared in any area in which "the defense of the state, state security, or maintenance of public order" are threatened. An area can be placed under martial law in time of peace as well as during a war: in 1966 troops of the Dzerzhinskiy Division of the Internal Troops were sent from Moscow to Tashkent, which apparently had been placed under martial law as a result of a massive earthquake.

When explaining the concept of martial law and its many provisions, Soviet textbooks generally list the lessons and experiences of World War II. This is a standard Soviet practice, whether the lesson be military strategy, tactics, or even staff procedure. The paragraph below is typical:

> In the years of the Great Patriotic War, the Presidium of the Supreme Soviet of the U.S.S.R. by order dated June 22, 1941, introduced martial law into a number of union republics and *oblasts,* and also on railroad, sea, river, and air transportation. In areas declared under martial law, all functions of agencies of state power in the area of defense, maintaining the public order and state security, were given to the military councils of the fronts, armies, military districts and, where there were no military councils, to the command of troop units located in the given area. Military powers were given the necessary authority for the carrying out in practice of the extraordinary measures. All agencies of state power, state and social establishments, organizations and enterprises were obliged to give every sort of cooperation to the military command in the use of local ways and means for the needs of the defense of the country maintaining public order and security.[14]

From the above it is clear that from the very start of a war in which Soviet territory might be threatened, the Kremlin leaders would declare martial law in those areas considered critical, and military commanders would be given full control.

Another Soviet textbook describes how martial law would govern the population:

> Martial law is a special state-legal regime, which is established under extraordinary conditions and which is characterized by the introduction of special (extraordinary) measures. One of the important features of martial law is the broadening of the authority of military power in the sphere of assuring the defense and security of the state and upholding public order. The right is given to the military command to take measures, provided for by martial law legislation, of decisive and merciless suppression of activities of spies, diversionists, provocateurs, and other enemy agents, purging the interior of deserters, panicmongers, hooligans, speculators, and other subversive elements.[15]

As will be seen later, rail, sea, and air transport in the Soviet Union is semimilitarized in time of peace. The textbook explains how requirements were met in World War II by the imposition of martial law, implying the same would be used in any future conflict.

> In the years of the Great Patriotic War the Presidium of the Supreme Soviet of the U.S.S.R. introduced martial law in a number of union republics and *oblasts* (provinces) and also on all railroad, sea, river, and air transport. This action significantly broadened the powers of the military command in areas where martial law had been declared.[16]

All functions of state power in the critical areas of defense and security were given to the "military councils" in various regions, or to the "higher command of troop units," as described by Lepeshkin:

> . . . In areas declared under martial law, all functions of agencies of state power in the sphere of defense, maintaining public order and state security were given to the military councils of the fronts, armies, military districts, and in places where there were no military councils, to the higher command of troop units located in the given area. The necessary powers for carrying out the extraordinary measures in practice were given to the military powers. In particular, they were given the right: in accordance with existing laws and directives of the government to draw in citizens to labor obligations for fulfilling defense work, guarding paths of communications, structures, lines of communication, electric-power stations, electric grids, and other important objectives, and for taking part in fighting fires, epidemics and natural disasters.[17]

In conditions of martial law, military rule is absolute, with all other agencies assisting the military commander:

> All agencies of state power, state and social establishments, organizations, and enterprises were obliged to give every sort of cooperation to the military command in the utilization of local ways and means for the needs of the defense of the country and of maintaining public order and security.[18]

How control would be maintained and the penalties for not obeying the edicts of the military councils are further explained:

For insubordination to the orders and decrees of military power and also for crimes committed in areas declared under martial law, the guilty were liable to criminal responsibility according to laws in time of war. Matters of crimes which brought harm to the defense of the country, encroachment on public order and state security, were handed over to the examination of military tribunals. In addition, military authorities were given the right to hand over for examination by military tribunals matters concerning speculation, malicious hooliganism, and other crimes envisaged by the criminal code of union republics.[19]

Numerous other Soviet publications of the 1970s, written for both military and civilian readers, provide similar descriptions of martial law, and of when and how it is to be used.[20] The Soviet people would expect that martial law, enforced as described for the World War II period, would be declared in the future, as required. They would see nothing unusual about its strict provisions or the authority of the military councils.

The "military command" that would be given authority to implement the provisions of martial law could consist of one of several types of forces. Among these could be units of any of the five Soviet services — Strategic Rocket Forces, Ground Forces, Troops of PVO, Air Forces, Navy, or units from other components of Ministry of Defense Forces, such as Troops of the *Tyl* (rear services), Billeting and Construction Troops, or Troops of Civil Defense. Other military forces that might be used would be the Border Guards of the KGB (Committee of State Security) or the Internal Troops of the MVD (Ministry of Internal Affairs). In the latter two cases, as will be discussed in detail later, the heads of both the KGB and MVD usually are four-star generals directly responsible to the Supreme Soviet, and are not under the Minister of Defense.

Provisions of the Soviet Constitution and military law indicate the basic mechanism by which the Soviet leadership would expect to control the population and economy in the event of a nuclear war. Whether or not this control actually could be effected would depend on many intangibles, such as the level of the nuclear strike, yields of weapons, and duration. Other factors would be the forces at the disposal of the military command responsible for specific areas, the capabilities and training of these forces, and the ability of personnel at various organizational levels to exercise leadership. Equally important might be the psychological reaction of the population, their perceptions of chances of survival in conditions of nuclear radiation, and the actual preparations that have been made by the nation for the possibility of a nuclear conflict. All this, basically, is the responsibility of the leaders of the Communist Party of the Soviet Union.

NOTES

1. R. Ya. Malinovskiy, Address to the XXII Party Congress, contained in *XXII S'edz Kommunisticheskoy Partii Sovetskogo Soyuza, Stenograficheskiy Otchet* [XXII Congress of the Communist Party of the Soviet Union, Stenographic Notes], Vol. 2. Moscow: Politizdat, 1962, pp. 111–112.

2. V. D. Sokolovskiy, op. cit., p. 306.

3. Ibid.

4. Ibid., p. 307.

5. Ibid., pp. 309–310. For a current assessment of the needs of mobilization, see N. V. Ogarkov, "On Guard Over Peaceful Labor," *Kommunist,* #10, 1981, pp. 80–91.

6. Sokolovskiy, op. cit., p. 323.

7. Ibid., p. 315.

8. A. A. Grechko, *Na Strazhe Mira i Stroitel'stva Kommunizma* [On Guard Over the Peace and the Building of Communism]. Moscow: Voyenizdat, 1971, p. 29.

9. Ye. V. Prokopovich, "Zakony Voyennogo Vremeni" [Wartime Laws], *Sovetskaya Voyennaya Entsiklopediya* [Soviet Military Encyclopedia], Vol. 3. Moscow: Voyenizdat, 1977, p. 375.

10. Ibid.

11. V. P. Fedorchenko, "Rekvizytsiya" [Requisition], *Sovetskaya Voyennaya Entsiklopediya,* Vol. 7, 1979, p. 102.

12. The new Soviet Constitution, called the "fundamental law" of the Union of Soviet Socialist Republics and adopted on October 7, 1977, specifically provides for the establishment of martial law in article 121, paragraph 15.

13. S. S. Maksimov, *Osnovy Sovetskogo Voyennogo Zakonodatel'stva* [Basis of Soviet Military Legislation]. Moscow: Voyenizdat, 1978, p. 58.

14. Ibid.

15. A. I. Lepeshkin, *Osnovy Sovetskogo Voyennogo Zakonodatel's-tva* [Basis of Soviet Military Legislation. Moscow: Voyenizdat, 1972, p. 102.

16. Ibid.

17. Ibid.

18. Ibid., pp. 192–203.

19. Ibid., p. 203.

20. See, for example, D. N. Artamonov, "Voyennoye Polozheniya" [Martial Law], *Sovetskaya Voyennaya Entsiklopediya,* 1976, Vol. 2, p. 218. Also see *Bol'shaya Sovetskaya Entsiklopediya* [The Great Soviet Encyclopedia], 3rd ed., Vol. 5. Moscow: Soviet Encyclopedia Publishing House, 1972, p. 224.

3
The Party–Government
Control Structure

The top Soviet leaders, whether they are members of the Council of Defense, the Main Military Council, or the head of an organization such as the Ministry of Heavy Industry, are first of all members of the Communist Party of the Soviet Union. They have reached positions of power because they are trusted members of the Party and have demonstrated some management capability.

The Communist Party of the Soviet Union is made up of approximately 17,430,000 members out of a total population of 265,000,000.[1] Of this number between 150,000 and 200,000 are *apparatchiki,* or "men of the apparatus," concerned solely with Party duties. Many of the top political members, such as K. U. Chernenko, also a member of the Secretariat, and G. V. Romanov, First Secretary of the Leningrad *Oblast* Party Committee, have been *apparatchiki* for most of their careers. The great majority of Party members, however, perform Party duties in addition to their regular work.

The Communist Party dominates all aspects of Soviet life, from industry to military science, technology, and even the arts and culture. Control of critical areas begins at the very top. For example, one Politburo member has responsibility for agriculture through the Central Committee department responsible for the same area. At the Central Committee level there are departments for Chemical Industry, Defense Industry, Heavy Industry, and the like.

The Soviet people today are told that their victories during the Great Patriotic War were due to the wise leadership of the Party. Therefore, in any future crisis, including nuclear war, the survival of the Party would be the primary consideration. If Party control should cease to exist, could the Soviet Union survive as a nation? This question has many aspects.

The Soviet Armed Forces are the Party's primary means of ensuring control. At times both the Minister of Defense and the head of the KGB are members of the Politburo.[2] The Administrative Organs Department of the Central Committee approves, and may make, key assignments and promotions in the Armed Forces. The Main Political Administration of the Soviet Army and Navy has the rights of a department of the Central Committee and is responsible to that body.

In theory, the Supreme Soviet of the U.S.S.R. is the primary control body. Again in theory, this is the body that would reinforce the Council of Defense, declare martial law, and act on matters of critical importance to the Soviet state. The "government" structure, from the Presidium of the U.S.S.R. Council of Ministers down through the ministries of the various republics, provides a framework for control. Men heading these ministries are first of all Party members. Their assignments to these ministries may have been due more to Party standing than to professional competence in a particular area. At the U.S.S.R. Council of Ministers level, most of the ministries are headed by members of the Central Committee.

The centralized structure of Party–government control, and the primacy of the Party, can be seen when examining these bodies in somewhat greater detail.

Party Organization

In March 1917, on the eve of the Russian Revolution, the membership of the Bolshevik Party, forerunner of the present Communist Party, numbered less than 24,000. In secret, the Bolsheviks began a process of power takeover by creating volunteer armed detachments at factories and in Party committees throughout the country; by November 1917, detachments of Red Guards had been formed in most cities. At the same time, Bolshevik cells in the armed forces were working at winning over soldiers and sailors. In November 1917, this small group of Red Guards seized power in the name of the Bolsheviks, and the War Ministry in Petrograd was reorganized under Bolshevik control. In January 1918, the

"Workers' and Peasants' Red Army," predecessor of the present Soviet Armed Forces, was formed.[3]

Party methods of maintaining control are exemplified by the method that Lenin and his followers used to ensure their control over the Red Army. The many former czarist officers who were brought into the new military structure were not trusted. Therefore, Party members known as political commissars, without any knowledge of military affairs, shared authority with military commanders. This provided for a dual command system, with all orders requiring the signatures of both the military commander and the political commissar. By 1926, however, numerous officers considered to be politically reliable had been promoted to higher ranks. At that time it was estimated that 40 percent of the corps commanders, 14 percent of division commanders, and 23 percent of regimental commanders were deemed qualified to become full commanders. The dual command system was gradually relaxed.

In 1937, however, following the massive military purges in which the majority of the senior Soviet officers were killed, the concept of the political commissar was again introduced, and *politruks* (political instructors) were assigned down to company level. This control was modified again in 1939, as Stalin's personal control over the Armed Forces appeared secure. In July 1941, when Hitler's attack and Soviet losses made it necessary to commission thousands of new officers whose Party loyalty was not known, the political commissar system was reinstituted. It was abolished in late 1942, after the main German drive toward Moscow had been stopped.[4]

At the end of World War II a massive drive was initiated to ensure Party control and indoctrination at all levels. In 1956, after Khrushchev's speech denouncing Stalin, Party leaders sought to ensure that Stalin, and not the Party itself, be blamed for all the mistakes of the past. Marshal Zhukov, who had been appointed Minister of Defense in 1955, wanted to make the professional officers preeminent in purely military matters and to lessen the power and authority of political officers. One of his rulings on Party matters within the military structure was that no political officer could hold a rank higher than colonel.[5] Whether Khrushchev was worried about the popularity of Zhukov or other Party leaders were concerned that their hold over the military might be threatened, Zhukov was removed from office in 1957 and became a nonperson. Since that time Party leaders have given continuing attention to ensuring that their hold over the military would never again be questioned.

Internal Structure

The Communist Party of the Soviet Union consists of 16,732,408 full members and 698,005 candidates (as of January 1, 1981). According to Soviet figures, 43.4 percent of these are "workers," 12.8 percent are peasants, and 43.8 percent are white-collar, primarily clerical, personnel. Approximately 26.5 percent of the members are women.[6]

As noted earlier, probably fewer than 200,000, or slightly over 1 percent of the Party members, are engaged full-time in Party duties. The remainder are expected to give all of their free time and energies to Party work. Although the work is hard, the rewards are great. Party membership brings better housing, promotions at one's regular job, and other benefits.

The Party seeks to attract the more educated elements of the population. For example, of 34,600 PhDs in the Soviet Union, 26,181 are Party members; and 203,511 of the 345,000 who hold Candidate degrees are Party members (as of January 1, 1981).[7]

In theory, the ruling body of the Communist Party is the Central Committee, elected during the Party Congresses held every five years. During the 26th Party Congress held in 1981, 319 full members and 151 candidate members were elected. In reality, the ruling body comprises the Politburo, with twenty-odd members, and the Secretariat, which has ten or eleven members, five of whom presently are also members of the Politburo. These numbers often vary, according to political exigencies.

The heads of the departments of the Central Committee (Figure 1) have considerable power. Some are in the Politburo or the Secretariat or both. An outstanding performance may give others a chance at the Politburo, whereas failure can lead to an assignment

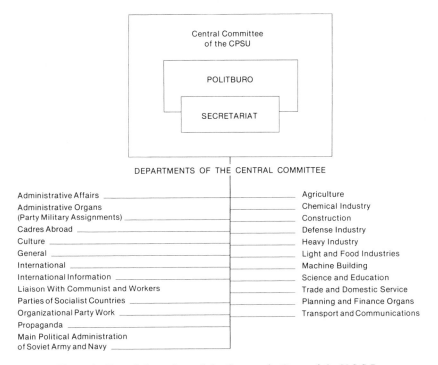

Figure 1. Central Committee of the Communist Party of the U.S.S.R.

to a remote region. A key control measure of the department heads is the authority to appoint individuals to the most important positions within their areas of responsibility.

Of the fifteen Union Republics of the U.S.S.R., fourteen have their own Party Congresses, Central Committees, bureaus (instead of politburos), and secretariats (Figure 2). (The Russian Federated Republic is the exception.) Below are the departments of the Union Republic Central Committees, corresponding in many ways to the departments of the Central Committee of the U.S.S.R.

In lower administrative regions, at the *kray* (region) and *oblast* (province) level, a "committee of the CPSU" is formed, which also has a bureau and a secretariat (Figure 3). Such committees also have departments that correspond approximately to those at the union republic and national level.

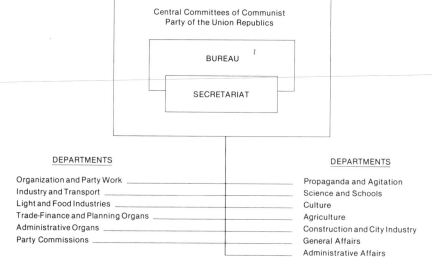

SOURCE: *U.S.S.R. ENCYCLOPEDIA HANDBOOK*. Moscow: Soviet Encyclopedia Publishing House, 1979, p. 176.

Figure 2. Organization of the Central Committees of the Communist Party of the Union Republics.

Any enterprise, institution, or other activity that has three or more Party members forms a "primary Party" organization.[8] In a major industry employing several hundred workers, the leading Party member in the organization would have considerable power, with all of the Party organs under his control.

Today's Party still operates with the secrecy characteristic of the illegal activities of the small Bolshevik cells active during the pre-Revolutionary period. Throughout the Soviet Union, Party organs are linked together with their own communications network. Instructions from the Kremlin may be sent in secret to Party secretaries at all levels, describing the positions that are to be taken on certain issues.

In order for the Party *apparatchiki* to advance up the ladder, they must attend a number of Party schools, the most prestigious of which is the two-year Party school attached to the Central Committee. The union republics and *oblasts* also have their Party

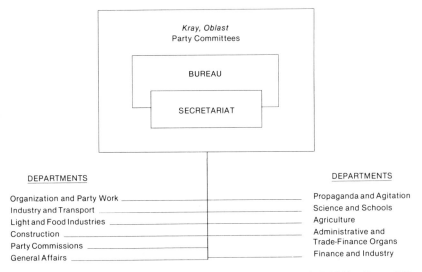

SOURCE: *U.S.S.R. ENCYCLOPEDIA HANDBOOK*. Moscow: Soviet Encyclopedia Publishing House, 1979, p. 176.

Figure 3. Structure of *Kray* and *Oblast* Party Committees.

schools, which prepare aspirants for positions of responsibility at these levels.

Would Party control over the entire U.S.S.R. cease to exist should the primary Kremlin leadership — that is, the Politburo and the Secretariat — be destroyed in a nuclear attack? Since many Politburo members are First Party Secretaries in union republics (i.e., Aliyev in Azerbaydzhan, Shevardnadze in Georgia, Kiselev in Belorussia, Kunayev in Kazakhstan, Rashidov in Uzbekistan, and Shcherbitskiy in the Ukraine), it would be unlikely that all would be in one place at the same time and would be eliminated in one strike. In theory, however, the Party's central committees in the union republics would remain the directing agencies, as would the committees at the *kray* and *oblast* levels. Whether or not these organizations would maintain Party control would depend on such factors as the capability of the Party leadership in the area; numbers, types, and reliability of the armed forces in the regions; and morale of the population. Important considerations might be how quickly communications could be restored between areas, and whether or not the Soviet Union might undergo another nuclear strike or be invaded by hostile military forces.

The Komsomol (The Young Communist League)

In the event of nuclear strikes and in the post-strike period, both the Party and the military command could call on those *Komsomol* members not already in the Armed Forces to assist in maintaining control. Although the 41.7 million youths[9] of ages 14 to 28 in this organization do not form a completely disciplined body, they have had some basic premilitary training, at the very least.

The *Komsomol* is an ideological and practical training ground for the majority of Soviet youth and also assists in identifying those individuals who are likely candidates for Party membership. *Komsomol* members are called upon to support programs of importance to the Party. This could mean volunteering to spend a year in construction brigades, working on the BAM (Baikal-Amur Mainline) railroad, or taking the competitive examinations to enter higher military schools.

Like many other Party organizations, the *Komsomol,* or "Communist Association of Youth," as it was first known, had its origin in the early days of the Revolution. In December 1917, the organization numbered approximately 15,000, and its first Congress was held the following year. During World War II the ranks of both the *Komsomol* and Party members increased, and by January 1944 *Komsomol* members in the Red Army numbered 2,223,000. Soviet writers today glorify their actions, attempting to portray each heroic deed in that war as being done by either a Party or a *Komsomol* member. The morale of the *Komsomol* was shaken in the 1950s after the disclosure of Stalin's crimes, but Khrushchev restored Party prestige with his re-glorification of the Party's role. Today, the position of the *Komsomol* is probably stronger than ever before.

The indoctrination of Soviet youth in Party concepts begins many years before entry into the *Komsomol.* In first or second grade the Soviet child is enrolled in the "Little Octobrists." Even the coloring books available at school portray the glories of communism and the Soviet Armed Forces contrasted with the evils of capitalism. At 10 years of age the child is expected to join the Pioneers, a 25 million-member organization whose many activities are supported primarily by the *Komsomol*.[10] In many Soviet cities, the "Dvorets Pionerov," or Palace of the Pioneers, is one of the most attractive and best maintained buildings in the area.

At the age of 14, Pioneers are eligible to become *Komsomol* members, although the majority of young men do not become *Komsomol* members until they enter the Armed Forces. According to Soviet sources, over 90 percent of men in the Armed Forces are members of the *Komsomol,* the Communist Party, or both. The head of the *Komsomol* stated in 1976 that 80 percent of the soldiers, sailors, sergeants, and petty officers and 20 percent of the officers were in the *Komsomol*.[11]

As Figure 4 shows, the *Komsomol* organization is similar to that of the Party. Most official positions are held by members older than 28. (The present First Secretary of the *Komsomol,* B. N. Pastukhov, born in 1933, was 49 when reelected in 1982 and has been a Party member since 1959.) Most *Komsomol* activities are managed by ambitious youths who either hold full-time jobs or are students. Leaders in the *Komsomol* are members of the Soviet elite, ready to enter key Party positions.

Professional Union of the U.S.S.R. (Profsoyuz)

The over 17 million members of the Commmunist Party of the Soviet Union form only a small percentage of that nation's adult population. To help control the total population other organizations are needed. The largest of these is the *Profsoyuz,* with approximately 128 million members.[12] It is the largest societal body in the Soviet Union, and it theoretically unifies blue- and white-collar workers.

There are now 29 different professional unions in the U.S.S.R., organized along production lines — aviation and defense indus-

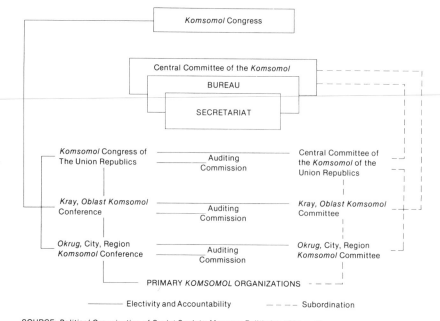

SOURCE: *Political Organization of Soviet Society*. Moscow: Politizdat, 1972, p. 61.

Figure 4. Organization of the *Komsomol*.

tries, railroad transport workers, coal miners, etc. All come under the *Profsoyuz,* which is directed by the All-Union Central Council of Professional Unions (VTSSPS). This council has 304 members and 105 candidate members, elected at the Professional Union Congress. Daily work of the Central Council is done by its Secretariat.

Unlike trade unions in the West, the *Profsoyuz* is an integral part of the Soviet control structure. All its activities are carried out under the leadership of the Communist Party of the Soviet Union.[13] Key appointments are made and approved through Party channels; the "Congress" that "elects" the members of the All-Union Central Council merely ratifies names previously given by the Party.

A major purpose of the *Profsoyuz* is to have its members strive to fulfill the five-year plans of the Communist Party. Another is to seek ties with trade unions in other countries and to make such foreign unions support the interests of the CPSU. In 1980, the *Profsoyuz* had contacts with trade unions in 130 nations.[14] (The leadership of the United States AFL-CIO is fully aware of the purposes of the Soviet so-called trade unions, and generally has been ahead of most United States government agencies in understanding Soviet intentions.)

The chiefs of the *Profsoyuz* are not individuals selected from the trade union rank and file. They are Party *apparatchiki*, as the careers of the present and past chairmen show.

From July 1967 to May 1975, Aleksandr N. Shelepin served as the chairman of the *Profsoyuz*. Born in 1918, he was the First Secretary of the *Komsomol* from 1952 to 1958. He was then reassigned to head the State Committee of Security (KGB) and continued in this capacity until 1961, when he was made a Party Secretary of the Central Committee. From 1962 to 1965 he was chairman of the Committee of Party–State Control. He apparently helped engineer the ouster of Nikita Khrushchev and was rewarded with membership in the Presidium (redesignated the Politburo in 1966). In 1967, he lost his post as Party Secretary and was assigned to head the *Profsoyuz*. Being relatively young (in comparison to other members of the Politburo) and ambitious, Shelepin may have attempted to make a premature bid for Party control. For reasons that are still unknown, he lost his Politburo seat in April 1975 and was replaced as head of the *Profsoyuz* the following month.

Shelepin's successor was A. I. Shibayev, born in 1915, a Party worker and factory director. From 1955 to 1977 he was Second, then First Secretary of the Saratov *Oblast* Communist Party Committee. He has been a member of the Central Committee of the Communist Party since 1961.

The *Profsoyuz* assists the Party in keeping its members and other workers in line, seeing that all edicts are obeyed without question. In a war situation it would help mobilize industry, train new workers to replace those called to active duty, and support whatever orders are dictated by the Party. It is another link in the total Soviet control structure.

The Government Structure

The Supreme Soviet

As already emphasized, the Communist Party is the actual policy-making and directing force in the Soviet Union. The government structure provides the bureaucracy that executes and administers Party decisions. Well-placed Party members are found in all echelons of this bureaucracy, and Party organs most likely settle disagreements over government policies.

The Supreme Soviet is the formal legislative body in the Soviet Union. Its members, numbering approximately 1,500, are "elected" for five-year periods. Individuals run without opposition and receive nearly 100 percent of the ballots cast. Exactly one-half are elected as members of the "Council of the Union" and the other half as the "Council of Nationalities."[15]

Approximately 40 percent of the deputies to the Supreme Soviet are reelected every five years. These deputies are leading Party members in the republics and cities, heads of key industries, KGB representatives, and top military personnel, including all commanders of military districts. Also elected as deputies to the Supreme Soviet are the chief of the Main Political Administration of the Soviet Army and Navy, his first deputy, and the chiefs of the political administrations of Soviet Forces, Germany; the Strategic Rocket Forces; and the Ground Forces. The chiefs of Civil Defense and GRU (military intelligence) are also deputies of the Supreme Soviet.

The 60 percent elected for the first time to a single five-year term include milkmaids, tractor drivers, and other representatives of the Soviet labor force. Such participation in government affairs by a wide spectrum of Soviet society is designed to help foster the illusion of a democracy. The biannual meetings of the Supreme Soviet are regarded as huge holidays for the participants. They are wined and dined in Moscow, and every attempt is made to make them feel that they actually participate in the affairs of the nation.

In addition to the Supreme Soviet of the U.S.S.R., the various republics and autonomous republics also have their own Supreme Soviets. Individuals elected to these bodies represent much the same variety of Soviet society as do those elected to the "all-union" body. Several thousand military personnel serve as deputies to the Soviets at the lower levels.

The actual functioning body of the Supreme Soviet is its Presidium. The Chairman of the Presidium of the Supreme Soviet is the formal head of the Soviet state, or "President."

The Council of Ministers

In the event of a nuclear war the Supreme Soviet would have little if any impact; even in peacetime it merely is for show and has no power. Its primary function is to "elect" the Council of Ministers,[16] which provides the actual management of the Soviet government. The Council is a cumbersome body, consisting of the following:

Chairman
First Vice Chairman
Thirteen Vice Chairmen
Thirty-three All-Union Ministries
Thirty-one Union Republic Ministries
Six All-Union State Committees
Twelve Union Republic State Committees
Three "Other Agencies"[17]

The All-Union Ministries are highly organized and directly administer various activities and subordinate groups, regardless of their physical location. The Union Republic Ministries administer some of their units directly but generally go through counterpart ministries bearing the same name in each of the republics.

Of particular interest to any military effort are the All-Union Ministries concerned with defense production. These are concealed under various titles, as follows:

Ministry	Actual Product
Aviation Industry	Military aircraft and helicopters
Communications Equipment Industry	Communications equipment, other than radio
Defense Industry	Conventional Armaments
Electronic Industry	Radar
General Machine Building	Rockets and space equipment
Machine Building	Munitions
Medium Machine Building	Military applications of nuclear energy
Radio Industry	Radios (civilian and military)
Shipbuilding Industry	Naval products and ships

Until 1977, the Ministry of Defense was a Union Republic Ministry, a rather difficult situation to understand in view of the centralized control of the Soviet Armed Forces. One reason may have had to do with mobilization, which is accomplished through the military commissariat in each of the union republics. In 1977, the Ministry of Defense was changed to an All-Union Ministry.

The Ministry of Internal Affairs (MVD), with its Internal Troops, is listed as a Union Republic Ministry, and an MVD general officer serves in each of the republics or large administrative areas. The Committee for State Security (KGB) was in a special category. Although a KGB general officer is assigned to each of the republics, the headquarters in Moscow appears to deal directly with subordinate levels. In 1978 the KGB was referred to as "the KGB of the U.S.S.R." (The MVD and KGB will be discussed in greater detail later.)

The centralized control by the various ministries may be one reason for the lag in the Soviet economy. However, efforts to decentralize the economy have been halted, since any decentralization might weaken Party controls exercised from Moscow. Indeed, it would be difficult to predict what might happen to the total Soviet economy if the central means of control were destroyed. While some individuals might work more efficiently if given a free rein, other industrial chiefs might be unable to function without direction from a central ministry.

In the event of a nuclear strike which destroyed the central government apparatus, such as the Council of Ministers and staff, control capabilities and economic restoration efforts should not be seriously affected. Martial law would prevail in areas that had been attacked, or in any regions where the population might be attempting to disregard orders of local Party officials. The important factor would be the effectiveness of the Party leadership at the republic and lower levels.

Insight for the Future — From the Past

Some insight as to how the Soviet control structure is intended to work in the event of a future war can be gained by analyzing Soviet writings about the "Great Patriotic War." Much of what has been published during the last decade is designed to provide the people with lessons of that war *that are applicable today.*

In May 1971, a conference was called in Moscow to look at the problems the *Tyl* (rear areas) faced during the war. Four prestigious organizations participated: The Institute of History of the U.S.S.R. (under the Academy of Sciences), the Institute of Military History, the Institute of Marxism-Leninism of the Central Committee of the CPSU, and the All-Union "Znaniye" Society. Findings of the conference were published in 1974 in a two-volume work, *The Soviet Tyl* (Rear Services) *in the Great Patriotic War,* under the editorship of P. N. Pospelov.

The first section of the book was written by D. M. Dukin, a Corresponding Member of the Academy of Sciences and deputy academic secretary of the History Section of the Academy of Sciences. He emphasized the complete control of the Party over all aspects of the war effort, and why such control was necessary.

The conference findings make no mention of martial law — apparently the measure was not found to be necessary except in a few areas. Could the control structure as described by Dukin be exercised in nuclear war conditions? The relevant section of the book is summarized in the following paragraphs.

The 18th Party Congress (March 1939) presented the third five-year plan (1938–1942 inclusive), which accelerated the preparation of the country for withstanding attack. The Ministry of Defense Industry was allotted more than a fourth of total industrial capital investment. The Urals, Siberia, Volga, and Far East areas received special attention as the Party prepared for a two-front war.

In September 1939, the Politburo issued an edict "On reconstructing existing and building new aviation plants." In February 1940, the Central Committee ordered Gorky, Chelyabinsk, Perm and other *oblast* committees to assist aviation industry in every possible way. A short time later the Central Committee ordered aviation plant directors to report daily the number of planes and motors produced. In December 1940, the Central Committee and the SNK (Council of People's Commissars) issued an edict "On the responsibility of People's Commissars, directors of plants, and railroad chiefs for fulfilling orders and carrying freight for the aviation industry."

The design bureaus of the tank industry under the direction of Kotkin, Koshkin, Morozov, and Kucherenko built two new tanks — the KV and the T-34. The tanks were tested in the fall of 1939, and in June 1940 the Politburo took measures to ensure their speedy production.

In February 1941, at the 18th Conference of the Party, a directive was issued requiring the reorganization of industry for rapid conversion to wartime production. As a result, major economic, political, and organizational measures were implemented.

Within a few days after the German invasion on June 22, 1941, the Soviet state apparatus was reorganized to achieve maximum centralization within the political, economic, and military leadership. The Politburo decided to concentrate absolute authority in the hands of one extraordinary agency — the GKO (State Committee of Defense). GKO, headed by Stalin, was charged with carrying out the policies of the Party leadership. GKO decisions had the force of law — all Party, soviet, economic, military, trade union, and *Komsomol* organizations, as well as all citizens, were obligated to carry out its decisions. *GKO was a collective organ and all its activities were directed by the Central Committee, primarily the Politburo of the Party.*

In the first months of the war, extraordinary agencies of leadership were created in several cities in the immediate rear areas (Stalingrad, Sevastopol, Rostov, etc.). City Committees of Defense (miniature GKOs) were created in more than 60 cities to be headed by the *first secretaries of the oblasts and city committees of the Party.* Local GKOs had both civil and military authority and were military organizational and mobilization centers that directed all the activities of local Party, soviet, economic, trade union, and *Komsomol* organizations in support of the front. The presence of defense committees *guaranteed the necessary centralization of state leadership* and made possible operational decisions for all problems as they arose.

The Central Committee, its Politburo, and the GKO daily and purposefully effected Party leadership during the whole course of setting up and developing the war economy of the Soviet Union. The most important economic questions were decided at sessions of the Politburo and the GKO. Some members and candidate members of the Politburo, *being simultaneously members of the GKO,* were given general leadership authority for the basic branches of the war economy. With new emergency powers, almost three-fourths of the members and half of the candidate members of the Central Committee took part in the organization of the war economy, often combining this work with military duties. Commissions headed by Central Committee members and Soviet government members were sent out to implement operational measures in specific local areas. The Central Committee systematically received reports from central committees of union republics, *kray* and *oblast* committees, and made decisions on the direction of their activities.

Local Party agencies were given responsibility for development of the war economy; while reordering the economy and carrying out mass evacuations, the agencies transformed the entire country into a single military camp. These local Parties took charge of the economy in their respective areas. The establishment of "branches of secretaries of Party agencies," created by decision of the 18th Party Conference in February 1941, was broadened, and the number of branches and departments increased. As war industries began production, departments of aviation and tank industries, armaments, ammunition, and also departments of the most important branches of heavy industry were created and headed by secretaries of Party agencies. The institution of Party agencies of the Central Committee, union republics' central committees, and *kray* and *oblast* committees in enterprises considered most essential for the war economy was also broadened.

To increase Party direction of agriculture when communists and Party organizations were reduced in number, political departments were created again in machine-tractor stations and *sovkhozes*. These extraordinary measures helped the Party increase its influence in developing the economy and creating a strong, organized rear area able to meet the needs of war.

These actions took place when Party members were being transferred to the Red Army and Navy. Communists were the first to go to the front. In the first six months of the war, 1,100,000 communists went to the front — representing one-third of all Party territorial organizations. By the end of 1941 there were 26,200 primary organizations represented in the Red Army and Navy, twice the prewar number.

The general economic mobilization plan adopted for the third quarter of 1941 — drawn up by GOSPLAN (The State Planning Committee) and approved one week after war erupted by the Central Committee and the Council of People's Commissars (SNK) — initiated the first significant redirection of the economy. On orders of the Central Committee and GKO, GOSPLAN coordinated military production plans for all enterprises, and controlled matériel and technical support of war production. GOSPLAN received a daily progress report whose contents were recorded on a graph of fulfillment of war production.

The Central Committee placed a great deal of emphasis on ammunition production. On the second day of the war a *mobilization plan for producing ammunition* was put into action. Its fulfillment was directly controlled by the Central Committee of the Party through specially empowered workers of the Central Committee, who were secretaries of *kray* and *oblast* committees.

Finance was another high priority concern. Expenditures during the second half of 1941 were 20.6 billion rubles, more than double those of the first half. Money was obtained from taxes and collections, as well as from loans and savings. Manpower was also a problem in production: millions had been sent to the front. Of 31,500,000 workers and clerks at the beginning of 1941, only 18,500,000 remained at the end of the year. Iron and coal industries lost one half of their workers, construction one third. Recruiting new workers and giving them "political indoctrination" as well as production training became of paramount importance for military production. All were guided by Lenin's dictate, written in the Civil War years: "To the working front must be thrown all the able-bodied forces of the country: men, women, and even children."

In June 1941, the Politburo formed a Committee for Distribution of the Working Forces under the Council of the People's Commissars (SNK). This committee was given the right to give obligatory orders to all People's Commissars (*NarKoms)* and departments to distribute the work force in support of defense needs. Women, pensioners, students in colleges, and high school students were called to work in factories and plants. The proportion of women workers increased from 38 percent in 1940 to 53 percent in 1942 and 55 percent in 1945.

Work hours were altered. Overtime work was necessary, and vacations were cancelled. Workers could be moved from nonessential industries to war production. In December 1941 a stiff law was passed, preventing workers from voluntary departure from their jobs. A special order mobilized every able-bodied person not engaged in useful work for society. In 1942, this provided an additional 733,900 workers for industry, construction, and transportation.

One of the Party's most important measures in reorganizing the economy was the evacuation of factories, supplies, equipment, goods, and millions of people from the front areas to the interior of the country. This was done in a very short period of time. On June 24, 1941, the Politburo established a Council for Evacuation, and all Party and government efforts were concentrated on this vital task. GOSPLAN was ordered to devise a plan to utilize the entire reserve force of the country, including evacuated industries. It was necessary to keep each plant working until the last minute, and dismantling and loading often took place under enemy air raids. Hundreds of trains loaded with people and machinery headed east — over 1,500,000 freight cars.

Ten million people and 1,523 large factories were moved toward the Volga region near the Urals, to Siberia, Kazakhstan, and Central Asia. This massive operation created enormous problems for the reception areas. By working 14 or more hours a day, workers in the east helped set up the plants to begin immediate operation. By March 1942, the eastern regions were producing as much as the whole country had before the war. Three-fourths of all combat equipment, arms, and ammunition came from this area. Iron production had to be increased in the Urals and Siberia. GKO issued an edict in February 1943 that obliged all *NarKoms* to report twice a month on the fulfillment of orders for iron and steel production. The supply of fuel, raw materials, and electricity was to be guaranteed for war production plants in Sverdlovsk, Chelyabinsk, Perm, Kemerovo, Novosibirsk, and Karaganda. Rolling mills were soon in production.

Fuel production was critical to the war economy. Anthracite coal was needed after the Donbas region was occupied and the Mosbas was shut down. Areas occupied by the Germans had produced 63 percent of the coal before the war; the Kuzbas and Karaganda had to take up the slack. Production was scheduled to increase from 180,000 tons to 265,000 tons in six months. But this did not occur and production even fell. The Central Committee ordered Novosibirsk and Karaganda *obkoms* (*oblast* Party Committees) to work out effective measures, increase Party work, and meet production schedules or be severely punished. Workers from the Central Committee were sent to ensure compliance. Money was poured into the area to improve living and working conditions, and pay was increased. Later the Donbas was recaptured and put into immediate operation, which helped to solve the fuel problem.

Oil production also decreased after the beginning of the war as wells were shut down in the threatened areas. A second area had to be opened in the Ural–Volga regions. Equipment and workers were brought in from Baku to increase production.

The need for an adequate electrical energy supply became acute as industry moved east. Existing stations were expanded, and new ones were built. With more efficient use of power, the needs of the area were met. The Central Committee, GKO, and SNK concentrated on restoring electricity to areas as they were liberated from the Germans.

All branches of heavy industry took successful measures to ensure military production. Undergoing actual wartime testing, aircraft and tanks improved qualitatively as well. The T-34 tank became a legend. Production cycles were shortened. The Soviet Union, according to the 1974 volume, produced 3.2 times as many aircraft, 6.3 times as many tanks, and 7.7 times as many guns as the United States at the time. (Claims like this in a book supposedly issued by Soviet scholars probably deserve refutation.)

Agricultural production became a critical problem as the best agricultural areas of the country were occupied by the Germans, and in 1942, 4 million city dwellers were sent out to help bring in the harvest.

All this required maximum utilization of transport facilities. In June 1941, the Politburo gave first priority to troop and equipment transport. A fully empowered People's Commissar (*NarKom)* of Railroads was named for each front and given broad rights. Half of the country's railroads were in German-occupied territory. However, only 20 percent of the rolling stock was lost. But qualified workers were lacking, as many had gone into the Red Army, and fuel supplies were short. The Central Committees of union republics, *krays,* and *oblasts* were ordered to assist the railroads. In April 1943, by order of the Supreme Soviet, railroads were militarized, and in May, river and sea transport was also militarized.

The number of communists in war industries rose by 80 percent. During the war, territorial Party organizations took in 1,300,000 candidates for Party membership and 900,000 new members. On July 1, 1941 there were 3,817,906 Party members. In spite of the deaths of 3 million of this group, Party membership continued to increase and on July 1, 1945 stood at approximately 6 million.

"Wartime circumstances dictated the content, form, and method of Party and state controls over the economy," concludes the author of an article[18] on this subject in the work on the Rear Services.

Readers will rightly question the credit given above to the initiatives of the Communist Party and to the efficiency of the government structure. Soviet history has been rewritten many times. In the Khrushchev period the Soviet reverses during World War II were laid to Stalin's excesses. After Brezhnev came to power there was a continuing effort to glorify Stalin and to regard him as an outstanding leader in time of war. The initial defeats of the Soviets either were not mentioned or were simply glossed over. In all cases, however, both in the Khrushchev and Brezhnev years, the primacy of the Party continued to be stressed.

The central question remains. If the centralized Party structure is destroyed or if it cannot communicate with the remainder of the nation, is Soviet nationalism sufficiently strong to keep the nation together? As will be shown in the following chapters, the Soviet military structure could be a decisive factor.

NOTES

1. *Spravochnik Partiynogo Rabotnika* [Handbook of a Party Worker]. Moscow: Politizdat, 1981, p. 488

2. Whether or not the Minister of Defense and the head of the KGB are members of the Politburo appears to depend upon their personal power, and the support of the Party's General Secretary.

3. S. S. Lototskiy, *The Soviet Army,* p. 25.

4. Yu. P. Petrov, *Stroitel'stvo Politorganov, Partiynykh i Komsomol'skikh Organizatsiy Armii i Flota* [Construction of the Political Organs of the Party and Komsomol Organizations of the Army and Navy]. Moscow: Voyenizdat, 1968, p. 23.

5. *KPSS o Vooruzhennykh Silakh Sovetskogo Soyuza: Sbornik Dokumentov: 1917–1958* [The CPSU on the Armed Forces of the Soviet Union: Collection of Documents: 1917–1958]. Moscow: Politizdat, 1958, pp. 406–409.

6. *Spravochnik Partiynogo Rabotnika,* p. 490.

7. Ibid., p. 491.

8. Merle Fainsod, *How Russia is Ruled,* revised edition. Cambridge, Mass.: Harvard University Press, 1967, p. 229.

9. Sovetskiy Patriot, May 23, 1982.

10. A. M. Prokhorov, ed., *Entsiklopedicheskiy Spravochnik SSSR* [Encyclopedic Handbook, U.S.S.R.]. Moscow: Soviet Encyclopedia Publishing House, 1979, p. 179.

11. S. Arutyunyan, "Lenin's Komsomol Reports," *Kommunist Vooruzhennykh Sil,* No. 4, February 1976, p. 24.

12. *Spravochnik Partiynogo Rabotnika,* p. 510.

13. Merle Fainsod, op. cit., p. 578.

14. *Yezhegodnik.* Moscow: Soviet Encyclopedia Publishing House, 1980, p. 24. The *Yezhegodnik* is the annual yearbook of the *Bol'shaya Sovetskaya Entsiklopediya.*

15. See *Constitution of the Union of Soviet Socialist Republics,* adopted October 7, 1977, Chapter 15, articles 108–127.

16. Ibid., Chapter 16, articles 128–136.

17. For a complete listing of the various Ministries and Committees comprising the Council of Ministers, see the Appendix.

18. See P. N. Pospelov, *Sovetskiy Tyl v Velikoy Otechestvennoy Voyne* [The Soviet Tyl (Rear Services) in the Great Patriotic War]. Moscow: Mysl' Publishing House, 1974. Pages 5–48 have been summarized here.

4
The Soviet High Command

In time of peace, the senior military leadership in the Soviet Union is primarily exerted by three bodies: the Council of Defense, the Main Military Council, and the General Staff. In time of war, the first of these bodies probably would be given powers similar to those of the State Committee of Defense (GKO) during the Great Patriotic War. The Main Military Council at the same time would be redesignated and reformed as the *Stavka* of the Supreme High Command (the *Stavka* of the VGK).

Present Kremlin leaders appear to find in these organizations the basis for an optimum command and control structure. Their origins date back to the days of the Revolution and the Civil War. Contemporary Soviet writers describe the work of these bodies during the Great Patriotic War in a manner that suggests they will continue in the future. Since 1960 the control structure has been modified to encompass civil defense and other requirements of the nuclear era.

The Council of Defense

The forerunner of the Council of Defense (*Sovyet Oborony)* was the State Committee of Defense, known as GKO (*Gosudarstvennyy Komitet Oborony*). Marshal Sokolovskiy's *Military Strategy* explained the importance of this body, both during World War II and for the future.

All leadership of the country and the Armed Forces during wartime will be accomplished by the Central Committee of the Communist Party of the Soviet Union with the possible organization of a higher agency of leadership of the country and the Armed Forces. This higher agency of leadership may be given the same powers as the State Committee of Defense (GKO) during the Great Patriotic War.[1]

The "higher agency of leadership" referred to by Sokolovskiy is the present Council of Defense. As with many major contemporary Soviet organizations, its lineage dates back to the Revolution. Its predecessor was the Council of Workers' and Peasants' Defense, formed in 1918. During a lull in Civil War fighting, when soldiers were put to work in factories and fields, the council took the name Council of Labor and Defense (*Sovyet Truda i Oborony*), sometimes called STO.[2] During the 1930s the STO became only a rubber stamp organization, and in 1937, while the military purges and Soviet military actions in the Spanish Civil War were in progress, the STO was abolished. Its defense function was taken over by a Committee of Defense, which became an organization with some power during the buildup of Soviet military forces that was taking place at the time. In 1938, a permanent Military Industrial Commission was established and placed under the Committee of Defense.

The Committee of Defense was first headed by V. M. Molotov, then Chairman of the SNK, U.S.S.R. In this capacity Molotov had roughly the same function as the present Chairman of the Council of Ministers. In 1940, K. Ye. Voroshilov, who was deputy head of the SNK, U.S.S.R., replaced Molotov as head of the Committee of Defense.

Within a week after the German invasion, on June 30, 1941, the Committee of Defense became the State Commmittee of Defense (GKO), with Stalin as its chairman and Molotov its deputy chairman. Other members were K. Ye. Voroshilov, G. M. Malenkov, and L. P. Beria. Later, N. A. Bulganin, N. A. Voznesenskiy, L. M. Kaganovich, and A. I. Mikoyan were brought into the ruling body.[3]

The Council's membership included a number of the most powerful members and candidate members of the Politburo. The Central Committee of the Communist Party, through its agency the Politburo, was, as it is now, the ruling body of the nation. But with Party Secretary Josef Stalin serving as chairman of GKO and with Politburo members on the GKO as well, there was no apparent conflict between the two groups. One military figure remarked in his memoirs that it was often impossible to determine whether a meeting was one of the Politburo or GKO.[4]

In examining how the present Council of Defense functions in periods of tension or would operate like GKO in time of war, it is most instructive to look at the operation of the Soviet high command during World War II.

In February 1973, *Red Star,* the daily newspaper of the Ministry of Defense, began publication of a series of articles about the work of GKO during World War II. This series, which ran until May 1975, told the Soviet public about the work of the wartime State Committee of Defense (GKO). In hindsight, it appears that these articles were to prepare the way for the disclosure of the existence of the Council of Defense in 1976.

GKO was responsible for directing the entire war effort, from mobilizing manpower, evacuating industry, and restoring industry in liberated areas to establishing the quantity and times of delivery of military production. Directives of the GKO had the force of law. All Soviet governmental, Party, military, and economic agencies were obliged to fulfill its directives without question.

With respect to the war effort, GKO assigned political-military tasks, gave specific instructions for improving the structure of the Armed Forces, and determined the general nature of their employment. Representatives of GKO visited the front lines and were even credited with directing partisan movements in occupied areas.

In certain areas near the front lines, GKO authorized the establishment of city councils of defense, called extraordinary agencies, headed by local Party secretaries.[5]

By September 1945, the Soviet leadership considered that wartime powers were no longer needed and GKO was abolished at that time, "by order of the Supreme Soviet." The Higher Military Council (*Vysshiy Voyennyy Sovyet*) was reintroduced with Stalin as its chairman. The Council appears to have remained in existence until the present Council of Defense was instituted in the late 1960s or early 1970s.

Analysts do not agree as to the full membership of the present Council of Defense. Based on several years of research on the activities of Politburo members most closely associated with defense matters, as well as on an analysis of the GKO during World War II, the following, as of April 1983, are believed to be members: Yuri Andropov, N. A. Tikhonov, D. F. Ustinov, and K. U. Cher-

nenko. All of these are Politburo members as well. Other Party
and military chiefs may be called upon to attend meetings, depending upon the matters discussed. Among these might be General V. M. Chebrikov, Chairman of the KGB, and General V. V.
Fedorchuk, Minister of Internal Affairs (MVD). Marshal N. V.
Ogarkov, Chief of the General Staff, may act as Secretary of the
Council of Defense.[6]

Article 121, paragraph 14 of the new Soviet Constitution gives
the Presidium of the Supreme Soviet the right to form the Council
of Defense.[7] In actual fact, establishment of this Council probably
is arranged by the Politburo, acting in the name of the Central
Committee. In any future war, the Council of Defense or its successor would be the primary ruling body and would have essentially the same type of membership as it has today. Its edicts would
be carried out through military councils in those areas in which
martial law had been established.[8]

Members of the Council of Defense are the most powerful individuals in the Soviet Union, and their successors also can be
expected to be so in the future. Their responsibilities are such that
they cannot give the greater part of their time to military affairs,
especially in time of peace. Therefore, a body especially formed
for this purpose maintains a more specific direction and control
over the armed forces.

The Main Military Council — The Kollegiya
of the Ministry of Defense

In time of peace "strategic leadership" — an expression used by
Soviet spokesmen — of the Soviet Armed Forces is the task of the
Main Military Council (*Glavnyy Voyennyy Sovyet*). This council
is immediately subordinate to the Council of Defense. Members
are believed to be Marshal D. F. Ustinov, Minister of Defense
(Chairman), followed by General of the Army Yuri Andropov,
Chairman of the Council of Defense, and the three "First Dep-
uty" Ministers of Defense: the Chief of the General Staff, the
Commander-in-Chief of the Warsaw Pact Forces, and the First
Deputy for General Affairs. Other members are the Chief of the

Main Political Administration and the eleven "Deputy" Ministers of Defense. These include commanders-in-chief of the five services, the Inspector General, Chiefs of the Rear Services, cadres, and Civil Defense, together with Deputy Ministers for Building and Construction Troops and Armaments.[9]

Based on current Soviet writings describing the structure of the High Command during World War II, it appears reasonably certain that in the event of a future war the Main Military Council would become the Headquarters of the Supreme High Command, or the *Stavka* of the Supreme High Command, as it was called after the Soviet Union entered the war.[10] To appreciate its organization and role, both in war and in peace, it is necessary to look at its origins and past performance. Even in this nuclear era, the structure of the Soviet Armed Forces is based on precedent.

A Higher Military Council (*Vysshiy Voyennyy Sovyet)* was set up and chaired by Leon Trotsky in 1918.[11] Later, as the Civil War spread over the country, the military councils in the field began to call themselves "revolutionary military councils." By end of the summer of 1918, the Higher Military Council adopted the name Revolutionary Military Council of the Republic, shortened to *Revvoyensovyet* of the Republic. It was directly subordinate to the Council of Defense. After the Civil War ended, the *Revvoyensovyet* was influential in building up the Red Army through its military reforms and the development of five-year plans for military equipment and manpower. The stated goal of these five-year plans was to achieve superiority over probable enemies in the decisive weapons systems of that time: aviation, artillery, and tanks.

In 1934, when the *Revvoyensovyet* was abolished, it was in large measure duplicating the work of the Committee of Defense. A Military Council with 80 members, acting merely in an advisory role, was formed to take its place. In 1938, the Military Council was split into the Main Military Council of the Red Army and the Main Military Council of the Red Navy, which corresponded to the two divisions, the Commissariat of Defense and the Commissariat of the Navy. This was while the military purges were at their height. The Party leaders were concerned that much of their military equipment was obsolete and had proven to be no match for the German aircraft and other military hardware encountered in

Spain. The Main Military Councils were given new responsibilities, and in particular were charged with examining what was needed to build up the Red Army and Navy, as well as with strengthening the defense capability of the entire nation.

In June 1941, the day after the German invasion, the Main Military Councils were replaced by the *Stavka* of the High Command, chaired by Defense Commissar Marshal Timoshenko. Stalin, Molotov, Budennyy, Voroshilov, Zhukov, and Kuznetsov were members of this body. Stalin rapidly consolidated his control: he became chairman of *Stavka* as well as GKO. At the same time he was Commissar of Defense and Supreme Commander in Chief of the Armed Forces. *Stavka,* once Stalin was at its head, became *Stavka* of the Supreme Command and finally, *Stavka* of the Supreme High Command.[12] This permitted extreme centralization and concentration of power in the hands of one man — Josef Stalin.

Based on present-day Soviet writings about World War II, it appears that in the future a similar concentration of power in the hands of one man is likely. The late L. I. Brezhnev's designation as Marshal of the Soviet Union and Chairman of the Council of Defense was an indication of this tendency. At the time of this writing (April 1983), Yuri Andropov has not been accorded these same powers; it should be anticipated they will come later if he is able to consolidate his power.

Through *Stavka,* Stalin was able to direct the war from Moscow. Again judging from current references made to that body, a new *Stavka* would take over the direction of the war effort in any future conflict. This would be the case regardless of whether conventional or nuclear weapons were employed and whether the war were limited or general.

In wartime, the *Stavka* would probably have only six to eight members: probably the Party's General Secretary (who would also head both the Council of Defense and the *Stavka*), one other Politburo member, the Minister of Defense (who also would likely be a Politburo member), the First Deputy Ministers of Defense, and the Chief of the Main Political Administration. There would be a board of permanent advisers consisting of commanders-in-chief of the services, other Deputy Ministers of Defense, and chiefs of service branches.

The role of the *Stavka* in any future war was explained by Marshal Sokolovskiy:

> The direct leadership of the Armed Forces during a war will obviously be accomplished, as before, by the *Stavka* of the Supreme High Command. The *Stavka* will be a collegial agency of leadership under the chairmanship of the supreme commander-in-chief.[13]

The Officer's Handbook, published almost a decade later, in 1971, confirms the role of the *Stavka:*

> Each service of the Armed Forces is designated for waging military actions primarily in one definite sphere — on land, at sea, and in the air — and carries out the fulfillment of the tasks under the leadership of the Commander-in-Chief of these services of the Armed Forces or directly of the *Stavka* of the Supreme High Command.[14]

To ensure that the orders of the *Stavka* were carried out, its representatives were sent out to the various fronts during World War II. If two or more fronts were engaged in either a combined or coordinated operation, *Stavka* representatives formed the necessary headquarters to effect the coordination. These representatives generally were the most senior Soviet officers, such as the First Deputy Commissar of Defense, Marshal Zhukov, or the Chief of the General Staff, Marshal Vasilevskiy. To coordinate the actions of two or more air armies, the *Stavka* would send the commander of the Air Forces or his first deputy to the front. *Stavka* representatives reported directly to their chief, Stalin, one or more times each day. Thus they supplemented the work of the General Staff, which was directly and solely responsible to the Supreme Commander-in-Chief.

Today the Main Military Council is sometimes referred to as the *Kollegiya* of the Ministry of Defense. It is important that this collegial aspect be understood when examining the Soviet High Command. Information is sketchy at best, but some data are available that describe this organization. For example, the first volume in the new "Officer's Library" series, *V. I. Lenin and the Soviet Armed Forces,* published in 1980, contains the following:

> The most important problems of military policy are discussed collectively at Party Congresses, Plenums of the Central Committee, and in the Politburo. There are also organs of collective leadership directly in the Armed Forces such as the *Main Military Council,* military councils of the services of the Armed Forces, military districts, groups abroad, and the fleets. Military councils collectively examine and decide all of the urgent questions of the daily life and activity of the troops.[15] [Emphasis added]

In 1972 a reference was made to a meeting of the *"Kollegiya* of the Ministry of Defense." In that same year an updated edition of the standard Soviet work, *Fundamentals of Soviet Military Legislation,* stated that:

> The most important questions of building the daily life and activity of the Armed Forces of the U.S.S.R. are discussed at sessions of the *Kollegiya* of the Ministry of Defense, which acts as a consultative organ under the chairmanship of the Minister of Defense, U.S.S.R. Members of the *Kollegiya* are confirmed by the Council of Ministers, U.S.S.R.[16]

In August 1977, *Red Star* again reported a meeting of the *Kollegiya* of the Minister of Defense, U.S.S.R. Looking at what appear as similar conditions in the 1930s, Soviet writings disclose that the *Revvoyensovyet* of the U.S.S.R. operated as the *Kollegiya* of the Peoples' Commissariat for Military and Naval Affairs. Based on this precedent and the context in which the Main Military Council and the *Kollegiya* of the Ministry of Defense are discussed, there seems little doubt that they are one and the same.

The new *Soviet Military Encyclopedia* does not have an entry for a "Higher Military Council." However, it does give the following:

> *Kollegiya* of the Ministry of Defense, U.S.S.R. A consultative organ of the Ministry which elaborates decisions on problems connected with the building up of the Armed Forces, their combat and mobilization

readiness, the state of combat and political training, selection, placing and education of military cadres and on other important questions. Members of the *Kollegiya* are the Deputy Ministers of Defense, the Chief of the Main Political Administration of the Soviet Army and Navy, and several other leading workers of the Ministry of Defense. The Chairman of the *Kollegiya* is the Minister of Defense. Its members are confirmed by the Council of Ministers, U.S.S.R. Decisions of the *Kollegiya* are elaborated on the principle of collegiality and are put into actions, as a rule, by order of the Minister of Defense, U.S.S.R.[17]

The above does not specify that Brezhnev was a member. However, based on the membership of the Main Military Council of the late 1930s, and on the fact that Brezhnev appeared with the *Kollegiya* members in certain photographs, it is likely that he was. In any case the ties between the Council of Defense and the Main Military Council (or the *Kollegiya* of the Ministry of Defense) are close. As already noted, the Party's General Secretary would be expected to head this body in wartime.

In the event of a period of high tension during which a nuclear strike might be expected, it is likely that the High Command would immediately move to hardened underground shelters in the vicinity of Moscow. Its ability to function would depend largely upon communications with various headquarters located throughout the nation.

Although Soviet writers emphasize the necessity for "strict centralization" of control, they also consider that it may be necessary during a nuclear war "to create main commands for leadership of armed struggle in the separate theaters."[18] The separate theaters could mean separate areas within the Soviet Union. This suggests an awareness of the possibility that communications with subordinate headquarters could be disrupted.

The General Staff

As previously noted, the Council of Defense has but few members, almost all of whom have major responsibilities in areas other than defense. It provides general strategic direction to the Main

Military Council, which in time of war would become the *Stavka* of the Supreme High Command. The *Stavka* is a body with very small membership as well. Obviously, then, neither of these two organizations is equipped to direct a major military force in time of peace or to plan for the conduct of military actions in the event of war. These tasks belong to the General Staff, sometimes referred to as the "brain" of the Soviet Armed Forces.[19]

There is no organization in the United States Armed Forces comparable to the Soviet General Staff. Its responsibilities and authority far exceed those of the Joint Staff in the Pentagon. Indeed, its nearest counterpart was perhaps the German General Staff as it existed prior to and during World War II.

As with the Council of Defense and the Main Military Council, the General Staff should not require basic changes to assume a wartime role. Soviet spokesmen describe the evolution and role of the General Staff in glowing terms. The Chief of the General Staff is the second-ranking officer in the Armed Forces, coming immediately after the Minister of Defense.[20]

Information about the actual work and organization of the General Staff is extremely limited. Many of the data available come from military histories and the memoirs of generals and marshals of World War II. Some of these appear to be describing an "ideal" general staff, and not the General Staff as it actually existed before and during World War II. It is likely that these accounts, historically inaccurate, were deliberately presented to illustrate how the General Staff is supposed to work.

As with most other Soviet military organizations, the General Staff had its origins in the Civil War. First was the All-Russian Main Staff, then a "Field Staff," and in 1935 the Staff of the Red Army was designated as the General Staff. After the Soviet Union entered World War II there were a number of changes in the staff structure, but on the whole it proved to be remarkably stable.

One of the most significant aspects of the work of the General Staff during World War II was the close supervision it maintained over all of the fronts. The General Staff acted as the executive agency of the *Stavka,* a position that made it possible to provide direction to all the Soviet Armed Forces from one centralized body. Stalin required reports on the fighting three times daily, which included a detailed map briefing each evening.[21] As already noted, the *Stavka* would often send the Chief of the General Staff and other senior officers to coordinate major operations involving several fronts.

The General Staff of the 1980s appears to be a direct outgrowth of the experiences of World War II. It has three primary directorates: operations, organization and mobilization, and intelligence. Other known directorates are military science, communications, topography, armaments, cryptography, military assistance, and Warsaw Pact matters.

The five Soviet military services are subordinate to the Ministry of Defense, with control being exercised through the General Staff. This same command line also goes to the sixteen military districts, to which are assigned units of the Ground Forces, Air Forces, and Troops of Air Defense. As will be seen in detail later, the military districts are important elements in maintaining control of the population in time of war or national emergency. (Commanders of the four fleets are subordinate to the Commander-in-Chief, Navy.)

Recent Soviet writings outline the task of the General Staff as ensuring

> . . . the coordinated actions of the main staffs of the services of the Armed Forces, the staff of the Rear Services, the *staff of Civil Defense,* U.S.S.R., the main and central administrations of the Ministry of Defense, the staff of military districts, groups abroad, air defense districts, and fleets.[22] [Emphasis added]

This places on the General Staff responsibilities for all the forces and activities of the Ministry of Defense. In the event of a nuclear war the General Staff would also be concerned with aspects of civil defense, both military and civilian.

Other responsibilities of the General Staff are more theoretical. For example, it also is charged with analyzing thoroughly and evaluating

> . . . military-political conditions which are taking shape, determine the tendencies of development of the means of waging war, the methods of their use, organize and train the Armed Forces, and carry out the necessary measures for assuring their high combat readiness to repulse aggression.[23]

This, apparently, would be one of the "brain" aspects of the General Staff.

Senior General Staff officers are carefully selected. Many have been in their positions for six or more years — many much longer — and have acquired considerable influence. Their professional loyalty appears to be to the Soviet Armed Forces and to the General Staff, rather than to any single service or arm.

The Soviet High Command is one of the most experienced military bodies in the world. Both civilian and military members of the Council of Defense reached their high positions only after years of proven capability for survival in Kremlin Party politics. They are accustomed to occupying positions of power and influence.

Although during the Civil War Red Army generals waged a few remarkably successful campaigns without direction from the Central Party apparatus, strict centralization of command and control is, and has been, a primary Party–military policy. There also were times during World War II when both military and civilian groups operated against the enemy without direct guidance from Moscow, but major direction of the Soviet war effort was given by a small group of men in Moscow. Even in time of peace attempts to decentralize Party power have soon ended with control being centralized more than ever before.

As noted, however, at least one Soviet theorist believes that a nuclear war might make necessary a number of main commands, and the organization of the Soviet Armed Forces suggests that, at least in theory, the Soviet Union could operate as many semi-independent units in a nuclear war situation. The following discussion of the Soviet military structure indicates how this might be possible.

NOTES

1. V. D. Sokolovskiy, op. cit., p. 361.

2. N. Vishnyakov and F. Arkhipov, *Ustroystvo Vooruzhennykh Sil SSSR* [Organization of the Armed Forces of the U.S.S.R.]. Moscow: State Publishing House, 1930, p. 101.

3. *Krasnaya Zvezda,* May 5, 1975. See also *Sovetskaya Voyennaya Entsiklopediya,* Vol. 2, p. 621, and *Istoria Vtoroy Mirovoy Voyny* [His-

tory of the Second World War]. Moscow: Voyenizdat, 1975, vol. 4, pp. 52–53.

4. S. M. Shtemenko, *The Soviet General Staff at War.* Moscow: Progress Publishers, 1970.

5. For an excellent account of the authority of GKO and of the establishment of regional GKOs, see P. N. Pospelov, ed., *Sovetskiy Tyl v Velikoy Otechestvennoy Voyne* [The Soviet Tyl (Rear Services) in the Great Patriotic War], Vol. 1. Moscow: Mysl', 1974, pp. 10–31.

6. There is disagreement among Western Sovietologists as to the actual composition of this body. Following Brezhnev's death in November 1982, the names listed are those believed by the authors of this report to be on the Council of Defense. Ogarkov's role is deduced from the memoirs of S. M. Shtemenko, op. cit., Book 2 (2nd edition), p. 500. When Shtemenko was Chief of the General Staff in the late 1940s, he said he also was Secretary of the Higher Military Council.

7. The same paragraph in the Constitution also gives the Presidium the power to appoint and dismiss the high command of the Armed Forces of the U.S.S.R., to proclaim martial law, and to order general or partial mobilization, etc.

8. This is another area not specifically discussed in available Soviet writings. The role of the GKO in wartime conditions will be discussed later in this analysis.

9. Actual membership in this body cannot be documented from available sources. A variety of sources, including comparable organizations in the past, indicate that individuals holding the positions listed are believed also to be on the Council.

10. "Stavka" is the Russian word for "headquarters." "*Stavka* of the High Command" was the designation when this body was headed by the Minister of Defense. When Stalin became its chairman, it was redesignated as "*Stavka* of the Supreme High Command."

11. S. S. Lototskiy, *The Soviet Army,* p. 42.

12. B. M. Shaposhnikov was named Chief of the General Staff on July 20, 1941, when Zhukov left to command the Reserve Front. Shaposhnikov was then included in the *Stavka.*

13. V. D. Sokolovskiy, op. cit., p. 361.

14. S. N. Kozlov, ed., *Spravochnik Ofitsera* [Officer's Handbook]. Moscow: Voyenizdat, 1971, p. 127.

15. A. S. Zheltov, ed., *V. I. Lenin i Sovetskiye Vooruzhennyye Sily* [V. I. Lenin and the Soviet Armed Forces]. Moscow: Voyenizdat, 1980, p. 184. A previous "Officer's Library" series of books was annnounced in December 1964, and contained 17 volumes.

16. A. I. Lepeshkin, op. cit., p. 91.

17. "Kollegiya Ministerstva Oborony SSSR" [*Kollegiya* of the Ministry of Defense, U.S.S.R.], *Sovetskaya Voyennaya Entsiklopediya,* Vol. 4, 1977, p. 235.

18. M. P. Skirdo, op. cit., p. 148.

19. For some of the reasons why the General Staff is called the "brain," see V. G. Kulikov, "Mozg Armii," [The Brain of the Army], *Pravda,* November 13, 1974, p. 2.

20. Prior to 1977 the order of precedence in the Soviet High Command was as follows: Minister of Defense; Commander in Chief, Warsaw Pact; and Chief of the General Staff. In early 1977 the order was changed so that the Chief of the General Staff came immediately after the Minister of Defense.

21. S. M. Shtemenko, op. cit., p. 140.

22. V. G. Kulikov, "General'nyy Shtab" [General Staff], *Sovetskaya Voyennaya Entsiklopediya,* 1976, Vol. 2, p. 513.

23. Ibid.

5
Forces of the Ministry
of Defense

The Soviet Armed Forces could be the critical factor determining the ability of the Soviet leadership to maintain control of the population in nuclear war conditions. They are ideally structured for the task in a number of ways. For example, the Soviet Union is divided into sixteen military districts, each with a sizeable staff and with both ground and air operational units. For war planning purposes, the nation may be further divided into five continental theaters of military operations, each of which would encompass several military districts. Should the primary requirement of the CPSU be to control the population in areas that had undergone nuclear attack, martial law could be declared, and military commanders could implement the necessary measures.

Virtually all able-bodied Soviet males could quickly be mobilized for military purposes. Under the provisions of the Law on Universal Military Obligation, approximately 80 percent of the male population is called up for active military service for a period of two to three years, depending upon the service assigned.[1] When their active duty obligations are completed, individuals are "discharged into the reserves." Even if an individual somehow misses active duty service, he still must be registered on the reserve rolls. Those in the reserve are carried on the books of the military commissariat until age 50.[2]

Approximately 1,700,000 Soviet young men are called up each year for military duty, and approximately the same number are released.[3] The Soviet Armed Forces have a reserve manpower pool of 8–9 million men under age 27 who have had active military service within a five-year period. As demonstrated by the mobilization of certain reserve units immediately prior to the invasions of Czechoslovakia in 1968 and Afghanistan in 1979, the reserves can be rapidly deployed.

Because of the structure of the Soviet Armed Forces, their capabilities for controlling areas in the interior of the nation during and after a nuclear strike may be considerably greater than those of the U.S. Armed Forces. Soviet military forces consist not only of the five primary services — Strategic Rocket Forces, Ground Forces, Troops of Air Defense, Air Forces, and Navy. There are other large components of military troops which are not assigned to any one of the five services but provide support for all. Among these are the Building and Construction Troops, Troops of the *Tyl* (rear services or logistic support), Civil Defense Troops, and a number of "special troops" — communications, engineers, railroad, road building, etc. These troops are trained and psychologically prepared to function in combat conditions, including those involving the use of chemical, nuclear, and biological weapons.

By Soviet law, the Border Guards of the KGB and the Internal Troops of the MVD are considered parts of the Soviet Armed Forces.[4] These are not para-military forces, as they are sometimes described in the Western press, but are full-time troops. The Border Guards of the KGB, and not forces of the Ministry of Defense, have been engaged in many skirmishes with the Chinese, including the 1969 Battle of Damanskiy Island.[5]

To show the potential role that the Soviet Armed Forces could play in maintaining internal controls in nuclear war conditions, the basic structure of these forces will be reviewed. Emphasis will be given to those capabilities that could most directly contribute to such a task.

Basic Structure

Figure 5 shows the basic overall organization of the Soviet Armed Forces. The following discussion mentions each of its components and deals in more detail with those that would be significant in analyzing control capabilities.

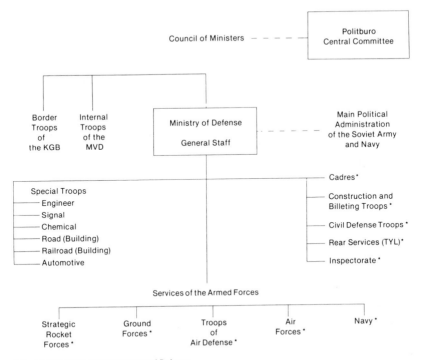

Figure 5. Organization of the Soviet Armed Forces.

Strategic Rocket Forces

Troops assigned to the Strategic Rocket Forces probably would not be a major factor in maintaining control. If their missiles were expended or missile launch areas destroyed, the survivors could be used for civil defense duties.

Navy

Naval units on shore would be disciplined bodies, which could either be absorbed by the local military commanders and used for enforcing martial law or used for civil defense duties.

Troops of Air Defense

This force is charged with providing warning to civil defense units. Its radars, interceptors, and surface–to–air missiles (SAMs) are located in thousands of sites throughout the U.S.S.R., often in very small detachments. These military units, if no longer needed against an external threat, could contribute to the pool of disciplined manpower.

Air Forces

This service is divided into three primary components: long-range aviation, air transport, and frontal aviation. In the event of a nuclear strike, air transport would provide much the same assistance as would units of military air transport in the United States. Frontal aviation units are assigned either to the military districts or to the groups of forces abroad.

Ground Forces

This is the largest of the Soviet services. All of its personnel are assigned either to the military districts or to the groups of forces abroad. The Commander-in-Chief, Ground Forces, does not have any units under his direct control. Ground Force units assigned to the military districts would be the most important single factor in ensuring control of the population during and after a nuclear strike.

Supporting Troops

As previously noted, large units of Soviet military personnel are not assigned to any single service, but come under the Ministry of Defense. These may number between 1 and 2 million men. Some are assigned directly to military districts, some to groups of forces abroad. The nature of the troops in special and supporting categories is such that they would be in a position to play a major supporting role in nuclear war conditions. They provide an infrastructure and are located throughout the entire territory of the U.S.S.R.

Construction and Billeting Troops

The Construction and Billeting Troops are headed by a Deputy Minister of Defense. The number of troops is unknown, although estimates vary between 100,000 and 400,000. When not engaged in the construction of military facilities, they may be used by other Soviet agencies. Many of the new buildings along Kalinin Street — the show street in Moscow — were built by these troops. Other examples of their work are Star City, home of the Soviet cosmonauts, and Sheremetyevo International Airport on the outskirts of Moscow.[6]

Members of the Construction and Billeting Troops go through the normal "beginning military training" required of all Soviet males and a brief period of military training after being called up for active duty. They have the same rights, obligations, and responsibilities as troops in other components of the Armed Forces.[7] However, they receive considerably less political indoctrination, especially during the summer months when outside working conditions are at their best.

The Construction and Billeting Troops appear to be a group of disciplined workers, under military control, who could be sent to critical areas as needed. This is the task they generally perform under normal conditions. However, there is a possible weakness or danger in the use of Construction and Billeting Troops in areas where normal Soviet controls might be disrupted. Although no figures are available, a high percentage of these troops appear to be composed of various Soviet nationalities, whose loyalty to the Soviet apparatus could be doubtful. They may not be fluent in the Russian language and could be unreliable for combat duties. Large segments of this group might be resentful of Moscow's control and might cooperate with any group seeking to break away from the Soviet structure. Nevertheless, under the direction of military leaders operating under the provisions of martial law, these forces should be of direct assistance in rebuilding critical facilities following a nuclear strike.

Rear Services (Logistics)

The Chief of the *Tyl* or Rear Services, also a Deputy Minister of Defense, is charged with the following functions: (1) finance, (2) fuel supply, (3) medicine, (4) military communications, (5) food, (6) military stores (trade), (7) clothing, (8) auto transport, (9) military veterinary service, and (10) the upkeep and maintenance of military housing.[8]

Some of the *Tyl* units are assigned directly in support of the various services. For example, the medical facilities unit would be organically assigned to Strategic Rocket Troop units. Other rear service activities come under the military district commanders. Like other Soviet troops, rear service detachments are scattered throughout the entire nation. The assistance they could provide the population during and after a nuclear strike is apparent from the functions they perform.

The rear services provide food to the military forces. Food is often in critical shortage throughout the Soviet Union, and the Armed Forces suffer the same shortages and disruptions found elsewhere. To facilitate food supply, the Ministry of Defense maintains military *sovkhozes* (state farms) whose management is assigned to the Chief of the *Tyl*. Since 1965 the number of such farms, located primarily in Central Asia, Siberia, and the Far East, has sharply increased.[9]

The amount of agricultural land controlled by the Soviet military and the location of the *sovkhozes* are regarded as military secrets. Percentages of the total food provided the Soviet forces by these resources are unknown. Photographs appearing in the Soviet press about military *sovkhoz* activities show both military and civilian labor.[10]

The auto transport component of the *Tyl* provides trucks, prime movers, and other road transport equipment, while another component provides the drivers.

Still another element of the *Tyl,* VOSO (General Administration of Military Communications [transport]), is responsible for planning and organizing the movement of all military supplies. VOSO offices are located in many of the larger railway stations, at river ports, and at airfields. VOSO personnel are knowledgeable about rail, road, ship, and air transport systems and capabilities of the entire nation. Such information would be indispensable to military commanders enforcing the provisions of martial law and seeking to restore services following a nuclear strike.

The Chief of the *Tyl* is also responsible for the maintenance of the "untouchable reserves" of the Ministry of Defense. (Actual guarding of the "untouchable reserve" stockpile might be assigned to the KGB.) Some of these reserves are foodstuffs. The untouchable reserves are also "of other types — various military supplies, weapons, and ammunition."[11]

Whether or not the Soviet Armed Forces, and perhaps large segments of the population as well, could survive the first few weeks of a nuclear war would be influenced to a considerable degree by the work of the Chief of the *Tyl*. As shown above, his responsibilities include the positioning of supplies, including foodstuffs, for future war. These duties are a part of the total Soviet effort in preparing for "the eventuality of a nuclear war."

Troops of Civil Defense

All civil defense activities in the Soviet Union are the responsibility of the Chief of Civil Defense, who also is a Deputy Minister of Defense. Civil Defense Troops are assigned directly within a military district and would answer to its commander. Because of the attention the Soviet leadership pays to civil defense and its particular status, both its civilian and military components will be explained in detail later.

Special Troops

Soviet writings refer to signal, engineer, chemical, road construction, automotive, and railroad troops as "special troops." Each of these services has its own chief who is responsible to the Minister of Defense. The activities of all are coordinated by the General Staff. Some of these troops are organizationally assigned to individual services; others provide a common service for all of the forces. All would be capable of providing direct and significant help both during nuclear strikes and in later reconstruction work.

Chemical Troops

A primary purpose of the chemical troops is to provide defense against chemical, nuclear, and bacteriological weapons. Specific work includes "radiation and chemical reconnaissance, control over radioactive irradiation of personnel, processing of troops, degasification and disinfecting of the area," and other special measures.[12] Obviously, their primary and initial responsibilities would be to military units. However, these troops should possess skills and training that would be useful in supervising civilian personnel utilized in restoring the economy and population centers.

It is important to note that the Soviet leadership gives serious consideration to the possibility of warfare in a contaminated environment. During the 1973 Mideast conflict, captured Soviet military equipment demonstrated that tanks, personnel carriers, and even clothing were designed for nuclear, chemical, and bacteriological conditions. Some photographs of Soviet military personnel show soldiers wearing gas masks while performing various tasks.

Officers of the chemical troops are educated and commissioned in three higher military schools, each of which provides a four-year course. Two are described as "higher military command schools[13] for chemical defense," and the third is a "higher military engineering school of chemical defense." Professional training and education are given at the Timoshenko Military Academy of Chemical Defense in Moscow. Students at the Academy "undergo training in specially equipped camps," and "instructors and scientists take an active part in improving and creating new means of protecting troops from weapons of mass destruction." Also at the Academy "a great deal of theoretical research of the scientists has not only defense significance but also *significance for the national economy.*" [Emphasis added][14] The Academy works closely with academicians and corresponding members of the Academy of Sciences.

The chemical troops provide a resource to the Party leadership that would be of vital importance in nuclear war conditions. Should Soviet troops not be deployed outside of Soviet territory, chemical troops would be in a position to work closely with civil defense forces and other groups seeking to restore the economy and to lessen the impact of radiation upon the population.

Signal Troops

The Soviet Armed Forces maintain an extensive communications network. Eleven "higher military schools" graduate cadets as officers to direct this massive complex. Many types of communications are available to military forces, from buried underground cable to sophisticated systems of the most modern design.

Signal troops of the Armed Forces appear to work closely with personnel of the civilian Ministry of Communications. In the event of an emergency the military and civilian communications elements probably would merge. Civilian students attend the Military Academy of Signals, the professional school for signal officers, and some of the civilian graduates have later "made great contributions in the development of communications."[15] Apparently considerable research, both basic and applied, is accomplished by the Academy's faculty.

Communications are the critical element in command and control. The 1961 high-altitude Soviet nuclear explosions may have provided Soviet scientists with information that is not yet available to Western analysts on the effect of such blasts on communications. The massive Soviet military network, linking all military districts and operational forces with hardened Soviet command centers elsewhere, would be essential in a nuclear war environment.

Engineer Troops

Soviet engineer troops have been given a specific role and training for preparation of defenses against nuclear attack. Most of these troops are organically assigned to military units and in an emergency could be called upon, along with other military forces, to restore areas that had undergone nuclear strikes. They would be in a position to work closely with civil defense troops, with their tasks being directed by the military command charged with enforcing the provisions of martial law.

Railroad Troops

Railroad troops, operating directly under the Ministry of Defense, are engaged in railway repair, maintenance, and construction throughout the U.S.S.R.[16] Their work is coordinated by the General Staff. Numerous articles and pamphlets extol their contributions to building BAM — the Baikal-Amur railroad that will run north of Lake Baikal.

In time of war, the Railroad Ministry, already organized on a semi-military basis, would likely be placed immediately under military control, as was the case in World War II. If Soviet troops are participating in a land offensive, the railroad troops probably would be in direct support to provide movement to the fronts. In nuclear warfare conditions the railroad troops would work in conjunction with personnel in the Railroad Ministry, under the authority of the military command.

Automotive Troops

As previously noted, the auto transport portion of the *Tyl* provides trucks and other transport equipment. Drivers and mechanics for trucks, tank trailers, fuel tanks, ammunition trucks, and so forth are provided by the automotive troops. The auto transport service is supported by automotive repair shops, maintained and staffed by automotive troops.

Soviet military spokesmen emphasize that in a nuclear war the major communications centers would be likely targets for nuclear weapons. Therefore, Soviet strategists emphasize that the requirements placed on motor transport will be even greater than during World War II. Trained drivers, assigned as organic parts of both combat units and the *Tyl,* would be essential.

To most Americans, who take motor transportation capabilities and skills for granted, it might appear unnecessary to have special four-year schools to train young men to become officers in the automotive troops. However, the Soviet Armed Forces maintain four "higher military automotive command schools," which — like other four- and five-year higher military schools — award the graduates with both a commission and a degree upon graduation.

The Military Academy of Rear Services and Transport offers further professional education and training in its three-year course.

Road Troops (Construction)

A great many of the roads in the Soviet Union were originally constructed by the inmates of forced labor camps, as were the railroads. In the de-stalinization period of the mid-1950s, when most of the forced labor camps were abolished, the road troops were formed. Their function is apparently to carry out some of the essential military road building that prison labor previously had accomplished.

In general, road troops work on roads in military areas, or in areas that have primarily a military use. However, these troops often can be observed at work in areas that would seem to have no immediate military significance. This practice suggests that road troops, like other Soviet military forces, can be expected to fulfill any type of work required by the Party–military leadership. If martial law were to be established following a nuclear strike, the military command would direct their work.

Reserves

As in all other Soviet military components, reserve personnel have mobilization assignments that would enable all the types of Soviet support forces to be readily expanded. Reserve personnel whose mobilization assignments are in the support forces may be called up for routine training or for special maneuvers, in the same manner as all other Soviet reserve personnel. The latter was the case in 1968, when large numbers of Soviet support personnel were mobilized to participate in the maneuvers that preceded the invasion of Czechoslovakia. Truck drivers (including some of middle age), who had been driving trucks for civilian construction projects, were called up for maneuvers and within a matter of days found themselves in Prague.

In time of a major emergency, such as a nuclear strike on the U.S.S.R., the chiefs of the special troops — signal, railroad, road (construction), and the like — would be in a position to direct the work of their counterpart civilian ministries or departments. Under the provisions of martial law, there should be little delay in such a takeover or subordination. The basic elements are already in place.

Theaters of Military Operations and Military Districts

For wartime planning purposes the Soviet Union is believed to be divided into five continental theaters of military operations (TVDs). The exact areas encompassed by each TVD and the locations of the headquarters are not known.[17] In time of war the military district commanders would come under the control of the TVD commanders.

As previously noted, all units of the Soviet Ground Forces and of frontal aviation of the Air Forces, except those assigned to the four groups of Soviet forces abroad, are assigned to the military districts and are under control of the military district commanders. Units of Troops of Air Defense also are assigned to the military districts. The command line to the military district commanders comes directly from the Ministry of Defense, through the General Staff. If the headquarters of the TVD has been activated, the military district, as indicated, would come directly under the TVD commander. Administrative direction to ground, air, and air defense units comes from the commander-in-chief of the service concerned.

The division of the U.S.S.R. into sixteen military districts, each assigned combined arms units, provides organized, disciplined forces throughout the nation ready for any emergency, including the possibility of nuclear war. Under the provisions of martial law each military district commander could have extraordinary powers over the civilian population and the economy within his area.

Military District Functions

At the present time, military districts vary in importance and in the number of personnel assigned to the headquarters. Many of the headquarters are located in major cities, often on a main street. Judging from the size of the main headquarters buildings, as many as 3,000 personnel may work in the Kiev Military District Headquarters. These include personnel from the Ground Forces, Air Forces, and Air Defense Troops, as well as from all of the support elements — signal, chemical, motor transport, and so on. In Novosibirsk the headquarters of the Siberian Military District is much more modest. The main headquarters building of the Far Eastern Military District in Khabarovsk could provide office space for over 1,000 personnel. Other elements of this headquarters are located throughout the city. The Central Asian Military District, formed in the late 1960s during the buildup of Soviet forces along the border with China, has its headquarters in Alma Ata. This headquarters appears to be primarily underground.[18] It should be assumed that all military district headquarters located in or near city centers have alternate headquarters outside the city, probably underground and hardened.

Military districts are geographical commands. Most of the military installations within a military district commander's territory would come under the commander's control. These include military schools, most military storage facilities, and military garrisons. Exceptions are the operational units of the Strategic Rocket Forces, long-range and air transport aviation installations, naval shore units, and naval headquarters. Installations of the Border Guards and MVD troops are also exempt from the control of the military district commander. In time of war, however, all military means within a given area probably would be assigned to the TVD commander.

In time of peace the major functions of the military districts are housekeeping and training. The necessary military installations are maintained and the personnel housed and fed. Youths serving their period of military service are trained in military duties in whatever service and unit to which they may be assigned. A highlight of this training is the maneuvers, normally held twice yearly. At times maneuvers are conducted in conjunction with neighboring military districts, played according to a variety of scenarios. These often end with celebrations in local cities, attended by senior Party officials.

Each military district has its own frontal aviation and air defense. The makeup of the units provides a capability for waging combined arms battles, since chemical, signal, engineer, and other service troops also are assigned. (See Figure 6.)

MINISTRY OF DEFENSE
GENERAL STAFF

Military Council of a Military District

Commander (Chairman)
First Deputy
Chief, Political Administration
Chief of Staff
Local Party Secretary

———— Chief of Staff

| Commander of Aviation | Chief, Personnel Directorate | Chief, Political Administration | Commander of Air Defense |

Chiefs of

• Rocket and
  Artillery Troops
• Tank Troops
• Chemical Troops
• Signal Troops
• Engineer Troops

Deputy Commanders for:

• Combat Training
• Civil Defense
• Construction and
  Billeting
• Rear Services
• Military Educational
  Institutions

| Assistant Commandant, Paramilitary Training | Chief, Sports Committee | Military Prosecutor |

Figure 6. Organization of a Typical Military District Headquarters.

A number of military district commanders already have had experience in maintaining internal law and order. Normally, throughout the U.S.S.R. the local militias, reinforced by Internal Troops, maintain control. However, in tense situations, they may require assistance. During the food riots in the Rostov area in 1962, public discontent with the food shortage was such that actions of the militia and Internal Troops were insufficient to prevent demonstrations. Tanks from a nearby military district installation were called in and quickly stopped the protests. Several dozen people were killed. The surviving leaders were rounded up and afterward disappeared, never to be heard from again. In the event of a nuclear war, troops in the military districts could be expected to maintain order in the same manner as they have done in the past.

Party-Military Relations at the Military District Level

At the 26th Party Congress in 1981, four of the military district commanders — of the Far Eastern, Belorussian, Moscow, and Transbaikal Military Districts — became full members of the Central Committee. It is interesting to note that two of these military districts face crucial areas of China. Commanders of the Central Asian, Leningrad, and Turkestan Military Districts were named candidate members. All of the military district commanders are members of the Supreme Soviet.

Military district staffs and local Party leaders are closely associated. By law, each military district must have a military council, which is the ruling military body in the district. The following are required members: the military district commander (chairman), his first deputy, the chief of the political administration, the chief of staff, and the secretary of the local Communist Party.[19] An example of such a military council can be seen in the makeup of that of the Belorussian Military District (as of January 29, 1981).

Commander General of the Army Ye. F. Ivanovskiy
First Deputy Commander General-Lieutenant Tanks A. I. Semirenko
Chief Political Officer General-Colonel A. V. Debalyuk
Chief of Staff General-Lieutenant I. Gashkov
Party Secretary of Belorussia T. Ya. Kiselev

In turn, General Ivanovskiy was a member of the Bureau of the Communist Party of Belorussia, and many of his officers serve on the Belorussian Party's Central Committee. This pattern is standard throughout the U.S.S.R. General of the Army I. A. Gerasimov, Commander of the Kiev Military District, serves on the Bureau of the Communist Party of the Ukraine, as do many of his officers.

Relationships between senior military personnel in a military district and local Party officials extend to practical matters. For example, if labor is in short supply during a grain harvest, the Party secretary may ask the military district commander for assistance. Thousands of youths serving their compulsory two years of military duty will then be assigned for one or more weeks of work in the fields. A military district commander may also assist managers of plants in his area with transportation. Construction and Billeting Troops assigned to a military district may be spared for work on a project required by the local Party secretary.

Prestige of Military District Commanders

Commanders of military districts are either three- or four-star generals. They will have had a wide variety of command and staff assignments before being given these posts. The only positions senior to those of the military district commanders are the Commander-in-Chief of the Troops of the Far East; the Commander-in-Chief of the Soviet Group of Forces, Germany; the Commanders-in-Chief of the five services; the Commandant of the General Staff Academy; and the most senior positions on the General Staff and in the Ministry of Defense.

It is often overlooked that the key figures in the Soviet Armed Forces themselves represent a significant part of the Communist Party's power elite. Generals and admirals in the military districts and fleets serve as members of the politburos and central committees in the various cities, regions, and republics. The very top military leaders are members of the Central Committee of the Communist Party of the Soviet Union. This "two-hat" development long has given the military arm a voice in Party circles. Control of the nation during and after a nuclear strike would remain within the customary Party–military apparatus, as it does at the present time.

As the above paragraphs indicate, the military districts have an ideal configuration for maintaining population control in the event of a nuclear war. They have the necessary armed forces, weapons, and training to quell any disorder, and they are familiar with the area and the local civilian authorities. As will be shown in the following sections, many other aspects of the Soviet military structure would facilitate the ability of the military district commander to enforce martial law.

The Military Commissariat

Throughout the Soviet Union there are military commissariat offices whose basic task is to keep track of all personnel and material within a given area that might contribute, directly or indirectly, to a military effort. The offices are controlled by the General Staff, through the commanders of the military districts on whose territory they are located. They are among the most important agencies of the Soviet military structure for maintaining control over the population.

In the event the centralized control structure of the Soviet Union were destroyed by a nuclear attack, the military district commander still would have the services of the military commissariat offices to advise him of available people and resources. The offices are found in cities, *oblasts, okrugs* (districts), *krays,* and *rayons* (localities). Military commissariats are defined as "local agencies of military administration" and also as "registration-mobilization organs."[20] More specifically:

> Military commissariats are the organizers of military work in local areas; through them close ties of the Armed Forces of the U.S.S.R. are kept with the sources of their formation and replenishing, with reserves and with the population. Military mobilization, registration and induction work, mass defense and military patriotic measures are organized and conducted by the military commissariat on the basis of close interconnection with local party and Soviet organs and social organizations.[21]

Among the basic tasks of the military commissariats are the following:

- Carrying out measures in preparing and conducting troop mobilization;
- Registering persons and economic resources in the interests of the Armed Forces of the U.S.S.R.;
- Preparing youth for doing military service;
- Carrying out induction for active military service and calls for study assemblies;
- Carrying out other defense measures envisaged in the Law of the U.S.S.R. on Universal Military Obligation and orders of the Council of Ministers.

Moscow, for example, has the office of the military commissariat of the Moscow *oblast* as well as that of the Moscow (city) military commissariat. There are smaller military commissariat offices in each of the 29 regions (*rayons*) of the city. In Vilnius there is the office of the military commissariat for the Lithuanian Republic, another of the City of Vilnius, and five additional military commissariat offices for each of the city's *rayons*.

Military commissariat offices for the *rayons* are often housed in small buildings, frequently wooden, that are identified only by a sign, "Military Commissariat." Although Marshal V. D. Sokolovskiy in 1962 stressed the need for all work associated with mobilization to be computerized,[22] it is doubtful that the use of computers has reached the military commissariat offices at the lower levels. Judging from the outside appearance of the offices, it appears likely that records are kept on handwritten cards.

Tasks of the military commissariat are simple yet vital to the Soviet concept of mobilization and military preparedness at the local level. The military commissariat offices maintain files on all members of the local community who are regarded by the authorities as having a military potential. Youths are listed by age, indicating when they are eligible for preinduction military training. The military commissariat office is responsible for ensuring that the beginning military training is accomplished, that physical examinations are taken, and that other matters affecting the preparation of youths for active military service are completed. Whether the youths are in school or at work, their whereabouts must be known at all times.

When an individual is discharged into the reserves after his period of required active training, he must report to the local military commissariat in the area where he resides. His records are maintained by the local military commissariat, who is responsible for notifying him when he is due for reserve training. The local military commissariat also keeps a record of his mobilization assignment, including the exact point to which he would report in the event of a call-up. If he moves from one area to another he must contact the local military commissariat office within a specified number of days, be entered on the rolls in his new military area, and be given a new mobilization designation.[23]

The military commissariat office chief and his staff work closely with local civil defense units, the Volunteer Society of the Army, Aviation and Fleet (DOSAAF), the Party, and the *Komsomol* organizations. Along with commanders of military units and schools, military commissariats support "local party and Soviet organs, *Komsomol* organizations, schools, institutions of learning, enterprises, *sovkhozes,* organizations, establishments, and *kolkhozes* in conducting work in the military-patriotic education of youth."[24]

All items that might have military use must be registered with the local military commissariat. These include automobiles, half-tracks, motorcycles, bicycles, skis, field glasses, and so forth. Construction equipment and agriculture vehicles also are registered. In essence, the task of the office is to ensure that all resources, both personnel and equipment, are known and ready for rapid mobilization at any time.

In a place where there is no military unit, the military commissar fulfills the obligations of chief of garrison. Within the limits of their authority, military commissars may give orders that are obligatory for all citizens, establishments, and organizations. They have the right to fine any individual for nonappearance at call-up by the military commissariat, for loss of military cards, and for failure to promptly report changes of place of residence to the registration organs.

The executive committee of the town (village) Council of Workers' Deputies, as well as heads of enterprises, establishments, organizations, schools, and *kolkhozes* must, "on demand of military commissariats, inform military-obligated and inductees of their call to the military commissariats and cooperate in the timely appearance of the call."[25]

There are no generally accepted figures on the number of military personnel in the Soviet Union working in military commissariat offices. Based on the number of identified offices in Moscow and Vilnius, and the regulations that apply to the establishment of such offices, it is estimated here that between 125,000 and 150,000 Soviet personnel are assigned full-time to military commissariat duties. Senior military commissariat officers identified in nine of the fifteen Soviet republics have all had the rank of general-major. The same rank structure has been identified in the autonomous republics, autonomous *oblasts,* and *oblasts,* with the exception of two individuals who are colonels.

In a highly mobile society such as that in the United States, it might be difficult if not impossible to maintain files of the type that are the basis of the Soviet military commissariat system. In the Soviet Union the task is less complex. All Soviet citizens, except for those in certain special categories, must have internal passports. These must be shown before a hotel room can be rented or before a job is assigned. Passports must be carried at all times. Young men of military age can be observed being stopped by the militia or Internal Troops and directed to show their "documents." The military commissariat, in conjunction with other local authorities, has a method of knowing who is leaving a given area and the names and addresses of all newcomers.

Soviet regulations state that during time of war the military-obligated and inductees are "forbidden to leave their place of permanent residence without permission of the *rayon* (or city) military commissar." On the declaration of mobilization, "all persons at that time in the ranks of the Armed Forces U.S.S.R. will be held in special situation." At the same time "military-obligated will appear at the place and at the time indicated in their mobilization designation on receiving the news or at the orders of the *rayon* military commissar."[26]

The work of the military commissariat is an accepted part of Soviet life. A major fictional work about World War II, Mikhail Sholokhov's *Fate of a Man,* written as seen by an ordinary Soviet soldier, describes the beginning of the war: "And here it is, war. On the second day a notice from the *voyenkomat* (military commissariat), and on the third, the troop train, if you please."[27] It is of interest that this soldier going to war was 41 years of age at the time and had a wife and three children.

During a period of heightened tension the military commissariat office would be one of the several agencies working with civil defense units to evacuate the city. It is likely that martial law would have been declared, and a military commander would be in control. Files of the military commissariat office would show who was to be mobilized, who would remain at work in a given area, and what portion of the population would be evacuated.

In the event of war, a sudden influx of refugees from a city or area that had undergone nuclear strike might overwhelm the local military commissariat office. At such a time, martial law probably would have been declared, and the military commissariat would have the support of other agencies of control.

According to Lenin, in a statement Soviet spokesmen frequently quote: "Without military commissariats we would not have a Red Army." The military commissariat worked for the Soviet leadership during the Civil War and World War II. The same system is certain to be maintained for the future.

NOTES

1. Soviet law carefully defines under what conditions an individual may be excused from military service. Those youths incapable of active physical duties are trained for administrative and related work. Based on personal observations and discussions with a number of Soviet citizens, it appears highly unlikely that over 20 percent of males escape military service.

2. A. G. Gornyy, ed., *Spravochnik po Zakonodatel'stvu Dlya Ofitserov Sovetskoy Armii i Flota* [Handbook on Legislation for Officers of the Soviet Army and Navy]. Moscow: Voyenizdat, 1970, p. 35.

3. In the early 1980s the number of Soviet youth (male) reaching 18 began to drop from approximately 2,500,000 annually. In 1985 slightly less than 2,000,000 will reach 18 years of age. An 80 percent call-up rate would place this number of personnel available for military service at approximately 1,760,000 in 1983 and only 1,520,000 in 1985.

4. S. S. Maksimov, *Osnovy Sovetskogo Voyennogo Zakonodatel'stva*, p. 48.

5. The major Damanskiy Island skirmish occurred on March 15, 1969, and involved perhaps 2,000 Chinese, opposed by a somewhat smaller force of Soviet Border Guards. Tanks, artillery, and armored personnel carriers were employed. See Stephen S. Kaplan, ed., *Diplomacy of Power*. Washington, D.C.: The Brookings Institution, 1981, pp. 274–277.

6. A. I. Romashko, *Voyennyye Stroiteli Na Stroykakh Moskvy* [Military Builders and Construction Work in Moscow]. Moscow: Voyenizdat, 1972. Various buildings constructed by these troops are shown in photographs throughout the book.

7. A. I. Lepeshkin, ed., *Osnovy Sovetskogo Voyennogo Zakonodatel'stva*, p. 58.

8. I. V. Safronov, ed., *Spravochnik Ofitsera Po Voyskovomu Khozyaystvu* [Officer's Guide for Quartermasters]. Moscow: Voyenizdat, 1968, pp. 14–15.

9. I. Kh. Bagramyan, "The Rear Service of Our Troops," *Yest' Stat' v Stroy* [To be in Formation]. Moscow: Young Guards Publishing House, 1967, p. 78.

10. Detachments of other Soviet military forces, such as those manning radar installations, are expected to raise "kitchen gardens" to provide fresh vegetables and some staples, such as potatoes. They also may raise some livestock, such as pigs, and keep a few chickens. In the event that food supplies were disrupted by nuclear strikes, outlying Soviet military forces would have the basic knowledge and resources to produce a part of their own food supplies.

11. V. K. Vysotskiy, *Tyl Sovetskoy Armii* [Tyl Rear Services of the Soviet Army]. Moscow: Voyenizdat, 1968, pp. 66–67.

12. M. V. Zakharov, ed., *50 Let Vooruzhennykh Sil SSSR* [50 Years of the Armed Forces of the U.S.S.R.]. Moscow: Voyenizdat, 1968, p. 509.

13. A Soviet "higher military school" is a four- or five-year school that awards graduates both a commission as a lieutenant and a degree equivalent to that awarded by a university. Students enter the higher military schools at ages 17–22, after passing a competitive examination, much as for West Point, Annapolis, and Colorado Springs in the United States.

14. V. Myasnikov, "Voyennaya Akademiya Khimycheskoy Zashchyty" [The Military Academy of Chemical Defense], *Sovetskaya Voyennaya Entsiklopediya,* 1976, Vol. 2, p. 179.

15. A. A. Frolov, "Voyennaya Akademiya Svyazi" [The Military Academy of Signals], *Sovetskaya Voyennaya Entsiklopediya,* 1976, Vol. 2, p. 178.

16. When traveling by train in the Soviet Union, one frequently can see these uniformed troops at work.

17. In the late 1970s the "Troops of the Far East" were established, with headquarters believed to be in Chita, east of Lake Baikal. General of the Army V. L. Govorov has been identified as the "commander-in-chief" or "*glavnokomanduyushchiy.*" Heads of military districts are merely called "commanders."

18. Histories of most of the military districts have been issued by the Military Publishing House of the Ministry of Defense.

19. A. A. Yepishev, "Voyennyy Sovyet" [Military Councils], *Sovetskaya Voyennaya Entsiklopediya,* 1976, Vol. 2, pp. 272–273.

20. A. G. Gornyy, *Osnovy Pravovykh Znaniy* [Fundamentals of Legal Knowledge]. Moscow: Voyenizdat, 1973, p. 90.

21. A. I. Lepeshkin, ed., op. cit., pp. 94–95.

22. V. D. Sokolovskiy, op. cit., p. 312.

23. For the basis of the authority of the military commissariat, see A. G. Gornyy, *Spravochnik Po Zakonodatel'stvu Dlya Ofitserov Sovetskoy Armii i Flota,* op. cit. Articles 12–22, pp. 29–30, describe responsibilities for beginning military training. Articles 80–104, pp. 40–42, describe how the military commissariat is to ensure the military training of those discharged into the reserves and how mobilization would be affected.

24. Ibid., p. 45.

25. A. G. Gornyy, *Osnovy Pravovykh Znaniy,* op. cit., p. 90.

26. A. G. Gornyy, *Spravochnik Po Zakonodatel'stvu Dlya Ofitserov,* op. cit., articles 92–101, pp. 41–42.

27. Mikhail Sholokhov, *Sud'ba Cheloveka* [Fate of a Man]. Moscow: State Literature Publishing House, 1957, p. 14.

6
KGB and MVD Control Capabilities

Background

The 1981 *Yezhigodnik* (Yearbook) of the *Bol'shaya Sovetskaya Entsiklopediya* stated the following:

> The Armed Forces of the U.S.S.R. consist of the Ground Forces, Strategic Rocket Forces, Air Forces, Troops of Air Defense, and Navy, forming the services of the Armed Forces, and also the *Tyl* (rear services) of the Armed Forces, staffs and troops of Civil Defense, *Border Guards and Internal Troops.*[1] [Emphasis added]

A 1978 textbook, the *Basis of Soviet Military Legislation,* described the Soviet Armed Forces somewhat differently.

> According to law, the Armed Forces of the U.S.S.R. are divided into four component parts: Soviet Army, Navy, *Border Guards and Internal Troops.*[2] [Emphasis added]

Border Guards are under the control of the KGB (Committee of State Security); the Internal Troops are under the MVD (Ministry of Internal Affairs). These armed forces, which are *not* under the Ministry of Defense, would be significant factors in maintaining control of the population in the event of a nuclear strike.

In addition to the Border Guards, the KGB also has other uniformed troops, such as the Kremlin Guards, and a system of secret police and informants throughout the U.S.S.R. The MVD controls the militia (police), firemen (who are militarized), and similar bodies. Personnel in the KGB and MVD, both uniformed and civilian, number in the millions.

How these two organizations might contribute to the maintenance of control of the population and the economy under conditions of nuclear war can be analyzed by examining their formation, growth, and present structure. Their organizations have changed at various times over the past sixty years, and they have been known by various names. On occasion the KGB and MVD have been combined. But their basic purpose — the use of force (and terror when necessary) to control the population — has remained essentially the same.

The history of the KGB and MVD goes back to 1917, when Lenin directed Felix Dzerzhinskiy to organize a force to combat counterrevolution and sabotage. A decree soon was approved for the formation of the All-Russian Extraordinary Commission for Combating Counterrevolution and Sabotage (*Cheka*). From the first months of the Soviet state Lenin used the *Cheka* for the deliberate practice of terror as a system of power. At the same time the *Cheka* was formed, the People's Commissariat of Internal Affairs (NKVD) also was created. In early 1922, the *Cheka* was renamed the State Political Administration (GPU) and subordinated to the NKVD. At the end of 1922, the GPU was redesignated the Combined State Political Administration (OGPU). When the NKVD was abolished temporarily in 1930, the OGPU was taken from its control. In 1934, the NKVD was reestablished.

By the mid-1930s, the NKVD, which had again absorbed the OGPU, was responsible for state security (espionage against Soviet citizens), Border Guards, the militia (police), highway administration, civil registry, and all penal institutions. It also ran major industries. With its four major components of control — the secret police, the regular police, Border Guards, and Internal Troops — the NKVD was a major power instrument.

The NKVD was the body primarily responsible for carrying out Stalin's purges, both of civilian groups and the military. Hundreds of thousands of people were executed, and millions were sent to camps where death was a certainty.[3] No segment of Soviet society completely escaped the purges; its victims encompassed peasants, factory workers, Party leaders, the military hierarchy, and the intelligentsia. Even the heads of the NKVD, one after another, were executed. This was a blood orgy much greater than even Hitler's execution of millions of Jews.

The purges drew to a close in the latter part of 1938. The next victims of the NKVD were the Poles. After the Stalin-Hitler Non-Aggression Pact of 1939, Soviet Armed Forces moved into Polish territory to meet Hitler's forces. The NKVD followed and designated hundreds of thousands of Polish citizens to be deported into the forced labor camps in Siberia. After Soviet military forces took control of the Baltic Republics in 1940, tens of thousands of innocent people were rounded up by the NKVD and sent to die in labor camps. During World War II the Volga-German Autonomous Republic was dissolved, and those of German descent were sent to forced labor camps or to the northern regions. The Crimean Tatars were uprooted from their homeland, and men, women, and children were scattered throughout the U.S.S.R. Thousands perished.[4]

At the end of World War II the NKVD continued its activities to ensure the supremacy of the Party and the absolute authority of Josef Stalin. Large-scale arrests and deportations continued in those areas of the nation that had been occupied by the Germans, especially in the Baltic states and the western Ukraine. The Chechens, a nationality group in the North Caucasus with a population estimated at 1,300,000, were deported as a body in 1946 to the Far East and Siberia.

Nikita Khrushchev's attempt to lift the lid and expose the horror of the work of the KGB and MVD for the Soviet people to see may have been a major reason for his ouster. In the late 1970s, the man primarily responsible for the millions of Soviet deaths, Josef Stalin, was being reinstated as a war hero and Party leader. The acceptance of human suffering as justified in order to keep the Party rule intact is a factor to consider when examining the ability of the Soviet leadership to maintain control in the event of a nuclear war.

In early 1941, the NKVD was split into the NKVD and the NKGB (People's Commissariat of State Security). In June 1941 the two agencies were joined, but were split again in December 1942. In 1946, each of the agencies was designated as a ministry, and they were renamed the MVD (Ministry of Internal Affairs) and the MGB (Ministry of State Security). Immediately following Stalin's death, the two organizations were consolidated into the MVD. After Lavrenti Beria was shot, the MVD was split into the

KGB and the MVD. In 1960, the MVD was abolished, and the KGB took over its functions. In 1966, MOOP (Ministry for Protection of the Public Order) was formed from a portion of the KGB, essentially from what had been the MVD. In 1968, MOOP was again designated as the MVD, with the responsibilities it has at the present time.

Yuri Andropov, appointed head of the KGB in 1967, was designated a Politburo member in 1973. In May 1982 he was assigned to the Secretariat of the Central Committee, with his deputy, V. V. Fedorchuk, assuming command of the KGB. After Leonid Brezhnev's death in November 1982, Andropov was appointed General Secretary of the CPSU. Shortly thereafter, Fedorchuk was shifted to Minister of Internal Affairs, with his deputy, V. M. Chebrikov, becoming head of the KGB.

The following two sections examine the KGB and the MVD as they existed in 1982.

The KGB (Committee of State Security)

In time of peace the KGB's primary responsibility is to ensure that the Party's control is not threatened. Abroad, its agents engage in espionage, terror, and other measures considered necessary to further Soviet policies. Throughout the interior of the Soviet Union, the KGB does not have its own military forces to enforce its measures. If physical resistance of any consequence is offered to KGB arrests, its leaders must call on the militia or the MVD Internal Troops. In a major uprising, such as the bread riots near Rostov in 1962, the KGB would call on support from the military district commander.[5]

The KGB, however, does possess its own uniformed military forces. The largest is the Border Guards, who number between 125,000 and 200,000. There also are other KGB uniformed troops about which little is known. The Kremlin Guards, who can be identified by the blue piping on their lapels and who watch over Lenin's Mausoleum in Red Square, are under the orders of the KGB. Other KGB troops control nuclear weapons stockpiles and other extremely sensitive installations. KGB troops also maintain

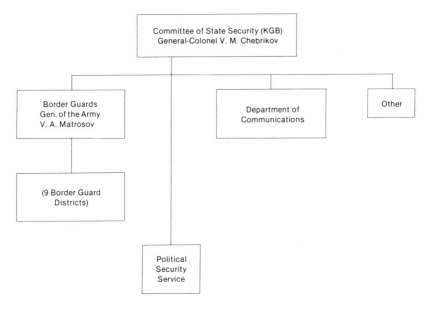

Figure 7. Organization of the KGB.

high-level communication links between Party organs. These communications personnel also are reported to maintain links between the Ministry of Defense and major military headquarters, such as the Soviet Group of Forces, Germany.

Border Guards, readily identified by the green piping on their lapels, are the best known KGB force. As noted in Chapter 5, the Border Guards, and not Ministry of Defense forces, fought the Battle of Damanskiy Island in 1969, and have been engaged in many other skirmishes with the Chinese. Each foreign visitor is checked in and out of the U.S.S.R. by these troops regardless of whether the travel is by aircraft, train, or ship. The Border Guards' primary task is to patrol the 60,000-kilometer border, which for purposes of control may vary in depth from 3 to 600 kilometers.[6] Nine Border Guard military districts administer the activities of these troops.

Border Guards are armed with tanks, armored personnel carriers, helicopters, and light aircraft. Units along coastal regions patrol in ships equipped with guns and depth charges. Such stockpiles are designed not only to ensure against unauthorized landings, but also to deter attempts by Soviet citizens to flee the country, even in rowboats.

Kursants (cadets) preparing to be officers in the Border Guards are trained in two "higher command schools" that offer four-year courses and award degrees and commissions upon completion. These schools do not differ in appearance from the four-year "higher command military schools" that prepare officers for the Ground Forces. Graduates of these schools, along with warrant officers and extended-duty enlisted personnel, form a cadre force. There is also a military-political school for Border Guard political officers.

Enlisted personnel for the Border Guards are provided through the Soviet system of universal military obligation and serve the usual two years of active military duty. Those aboard Border Guard ships serve three years, as do servicemen in the ocean-going portion of the Soviet Navy. After completing the required period of active military duty, Border Guard troops are "discharged into the reserves," a universal obligation in the Soviet Armed Forces. Those on reserve provide the Border Guards with a ready mobilization base.

In 1969, Soviet legislation provided that the KGB Border Guards establish a "military council" similar to those of the military districts under the Ministry of Defense. Since 1972 the Border Guards have been commanded by General of the Army V. A. Matrosov. He is directly subordinate to the Chief of the KGB, General-Colonel V. M. Chebrikov.

In the Soviet interior the primary tasks of the KGB are security and counterintelligence. Personnel working in these capacities number between one and five million. Many are under cover and are considered as full-time members of other agencies, and many are in the Armed Forces. In one form or another, KGB personnel are in all branches of industry, agriculture, transport, education, culture, and the Armed Forces — throughout the entire spectrum of Soviet life and activities.[7]

KGB personnel openly installed in military units or other organizations are not considered to be subordinate to the chief of the unit. They have the right of access to all of the department's or agency's files, regardless of type. In certain cases, local KGB personnel are authorized to take control of KGB units, local MVD Internal Troop formations, militia, firemen, and even Ministry of Defense military units.

KGB general officers are assigned in each of the republics, and in all major administrative units throughout the RSFSR (Russian Soviet Federated Socialist Republic), including the autonomous republics. Their work consists not only in directing counterintelligence operations, but also in watching the various Soviet nationalities, religious leaders, and any segment of Soviet society that might at any time question the Party's leadership. KGB headquarters throughout the U.S.S.R. possess excellent communications systems, which could supplement those of the Communist Party, the various civilian organizations, and the military.

In 1978 the KGB was designated "the KGB of the U.S.S.R."[8] The reason or significance of this still is unknown. It might have been done to place the KGB directly under the Party's General Secretary, giving him direct control of this key organization.

It is significant that the Border Guards are, according to Soviet military legislation, one of the four components of the Soviet Armed Forces. If martial law were to be declared in specific areas, it appears that the task of carrying out its provisions could be given to a KGB military command. Research accomplished to this date does not reveal any requirement in Soviet military legislation for the military commander enforcing martial law to be under the Ministry of Defense.

The MVD (Ministry of Internal Affairs)

As noted, the MVD and the KGB have been combined a number of times in the past, and may be again in the future. But in any event, the functions now assigned to the MVD will remain in the Soviet structure, basically organized as shown in Figure 8.

The Internal Troops of the MVD

Internal Troops are found throughout the U.S.S.R. For the present they must be regarded as one of the four components of the Soviet Armed Forces. Visitors to the Soviet Union, if they happen

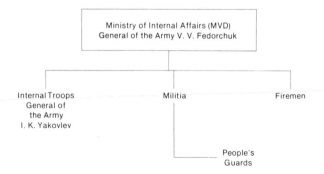

Figure 8. Organization of the MVD.

to know Soviet military insignia, will see Internal Troops, identified by the dull brick-red tabs on their lapels (somewhat darker
than the crimson red of the motorized rifle troops of the Ground
Forces), in all cities of any size. Except for the color on their lapels, uniforms of the Internal Troops are identical to those of the
Ground Forces and the Strategic Rocket Forces.

From the early 1930s through the 1950s, Internal Troops were
charged with guarding the hundreds of labor camps in the "Gulag
Archipelago," the details of which were not generally recognized
in the West until described by Aleksandr Solzhenitsyn. To guard
the millions of prisoners and the convoys conducting the victims
to their imprisonment and almost certain death, hundreds of thousands of Internal Troops were required.

Soviet spokesmen seldom mention the role of the Internal
Troops during the 1930s, but emphasize their role in World War
II. The following account, written in the mid-1970s, suggests what
these forces might be expected to do in any future war.

In the Main Directorate of the Internal Troops in April 1942 was
organized a directorate of Troops of the NKVD for guarding the rear
of the active Soviet Army. In May 1943, this directorate was separated
from the NKVD and became an independent Main Directorate. Troops
of the NKVD in close cooperation with troops of the active army up-
held order in the areas close to the front, combated enemy intelligence
and diversionary groups, took part in building defensive lines, evacuating industrial enterprises, guarding and defending important com-

munications, important objectives, convoyed and guarded prisoners of war and other persons judged criminals by Soviet courts. According to an edict of GKO on January 4, 1942, Internal Troops conducted garrison duty in cities freed from fascist occupation, helped the NKVD discover agents left by the enemy, and disclosed collaborators and enemy sympathizers.[9]

According to the new *Soviet Military Encyclopedia,* the number of Internal Troops at the end of World War II was significantly reduced. In actual fact, however, the primary reduction in these troops occurred in the late 1950s, after Nikita Khrushchev released millions of prisoners from forced labor camps. Although many camps remain, with guards provided by the Internal Troops, the number of prisoners is much less than during the Stalin era.

At the present time Internal Troops, often with fixed bayonets, may be seen guarding railroad and road bridges, tunnels, and other facilities deep in the U.S.S.R., over a thousand kilometers from any border. During demonstrations staged by the Soviet authorities before various embassies in Moscow, Internal Troops may be formed in side streets near the embassy concerned, in order to ensure that the demonstrations do not get out of hand.[10]

Internal Troops, like the KGB Border Guards, are equipped with tanks and armored personnel carriers as well as with light aircraft and helicopters. In the outskirts of cities, units of Internal Troops may be observed in small compounds, blending in with the local landscape. The compounds usually contain a barracks and two or three light tanks plus a few personnel carriers and jeeps. During drought periods when grain is scarce, Internal Troops armed with submachine guns may be seen in the fields as trucks are being loaded, and at storage areas where the grain is being held for shipment.

Cadre officers of the Internal Troops are obtained from the three MVD "higher military command schools," located at Novosibirsk, Ordzhonikidze, and Saratov. A "higher military school" of MVD rear services is located in Kharkov. As at other Soviet military and higher military schools, cadets are admitted between the ages of 17 and 22. Upon completion of the four-year course, graduates receive degrees and commissions.[11] A "higher political school'' for preparing MVD political officers is located in Leningrad. In 1974, the MVD opened its own military academy to provide advanced professional training for its officers.

In a manner similar to the services and arms of the Ministry of Defense, the Internal Troops of the MVD maintain a nucleus of professional officers, provided by the higher military command schools noted above. The Internal Troops also have warrant officers and extended service enlisted personnel comprising their cadre force. The vast bulk of the enlisted strength is made up of 18–20-year-old youths serving their required two-year period of active duty. As with other elements of the Soviet Armed Forces, these youths are "discharged into the reserves" when their obligatory military service is completed. The majority of these reserve troops probably are given mobilization assignments in the Internal Troops, permitting a rapid expansion of this force.

There are no published figures on the size of the Internal Troops. Estimates vary between 175,000 and 400,000. As the Internal Troops constitute one of the four components of the Soviet Armed Forces, military commanders in this organization would be in a position to enforce the provisions of martial law.[12]

The Militia (Police) of the MVD

The Soviet militia, performing a variety of police duties, is the basic instrument of public order in the U.S.S.R. One of its more observable tasks is that of checking to ensure that Soviet citizens are carrying their internal passports. Others include the inspection of automobiles and the control of traffic.[13] As a general rule they do not carry arms, although armed units can be summoned quickly.

The Soviet militia is *not* listed as a part of the Soviet Armed Forces. Unlike Ministry of Defense forces, KGB Border Guards, and Internal Troops, whose ranks are filled primarily by youths fulfilling their required military service, the militia is manned by individuals making this work a career. They appear to be local residents. Before going into the militia they already will have completed their military service obligations.

When called on to quell a local disturbance, such as an argument over the amount of a check in a restaurant, the militiamen may receive as much verbal abuse as do police officers in the United States. They do not seem to be feared by the ordinary Soviet citizen as a KGB Border Guard or even a member of the Internal Troops might be. There is no argument, however, when a militiaman finds an individual does not have his passport or has violated a driving regulation.

The Soviet militia is centrally controlled by the Chief of the Main MVD Militia Directorate in Moscow. The head of the militia in each of the republics, insofar as can be determined, holds the rank of general. *Oblast* militia chiefs normally are colonels. In major cities, such as Moscow, the chief of the militia likely will be a general officer.

The gray militia uniforms are standardized throughout the Soviet Union. The militia has its own political officers. As in all other organizations in the Soviet Union, KGB personnel keep watch in the militia for any sign of activity that might be considered hostile to the Party's control over the Soviet state.

In a period of high tension or a nuclear exchange, militia forces would support the military command once martial law is declared. In other cases the militia would continue normal enforcement tasks. At all times it is a significant force in maintaining overall control.

The "People's Guards" (Narodnyye Druzhiny)

In 1958, shortly after the millions of Soviet citizens were released from labor camps and the size of the Internal Troops was reduced, the "People's Guards" were established.[14] Theoretically they are controlled by local Party organs, but in practice they work in support of the militia. They are described as a "volunteer" force. If the normal Soviet "volunteer" pattern is followed, ambitious individuals are pressured into this activity as part of their *Komsomol* or Party obligations.

It is not known how many hours each week or month individuals are expected to devote to this activity. When on duty, "People's Guards" are identified by red armbands. They are very zealous in their tasks, especially when assisting in directing traffic.

One of their duties appears to be to keep a very strict eye on youth, especially those who try to adopt Western mannerisms. They have the right to detain individuals but do not have the right to make arrests. If arrest is thought necessary, the militia must be summoned.

In the larger cities the "People's Guards" generally are not armed. However, in border areas of Central Asia and the Far East, both men and women have been seen standing guard at tunnel entrances and on bridges, armed with submachine guns and wearing the customary red armbands.

In the event of population dislocations caused by nuclear strikes, the "People's Guards" would be an identifiable group to assist the militia and the armed forces in maintaining order. They represent yet another Soviet control apparatus.

Firemen of the MVD

In addition to the Internal Troops and militia, the MVD also controls the Soviet firefighting service. Firemen wear uniforms similar to those of the Internal Troops. They are commanded by a "General Internal Service Third Rank" and receive training in small arms, riot control, and anti-guerrilla operations. Practically all firemen have completed compulsory military service.

The firemen's organization follows that of a typical Soviet military organization, with battalions, companies, and platoons. They have their own political officers and are subject to the same rules as those governing MVD troops.[15]

During World War II, units of firemen worked closely with formations of MPVO (then civil defense). They were charged with the protection of transportation centers, warehouses, and other major installations.[16]

In 1968, the MVD had five "technical fire schools," and seven secondary schools had special departments for the study of firefighting equipment and security. MVD higher schools also have faculties for instruction in the use of firefighting equipment.

Industrial plants have volunteer firemen, fire prevention commissions, and fire inspectors to assist regular firemen. All are reminded that they must "be ready to protect the Motherland and to carry out the tasks of Civil Defense, since the firefighting service is one of its basic parts." Firemen maintain close ties with Civil Defense troops and agencies and take part in civil defense exercises.

The combined capabilities of the KGB and MVD forces to control the Soviet population are impressive. KGB agents and informants, with the Internal Troops, militia, and other MVD components in support, are able to contain all but the most severe disturbances. Their chiefs and senior personnel wear the customary two hats — those of ranking Party officials as well as of officers in their organizations. As illustrated in the following chapter, KGB and MVD forces are closely allied with the civil defense structure.

NOTES

1. *Yezhegodnik* [Yearbook]. Annual publication of the *Bol'shaya Sovetskaya Entsiklopediya.* Moscow: Soviet Encyclopedia Publishing House, 1981, p. 64.

2. S. S. Maksimov, *Osnovy Sovetskogo Voyennogo Zakonodatel's-tva,* op. cit., p. 48. The paragraph continues to explain further the Soviet military structure as follows: "The Soviet Army is divided into the services of the Armed Forces: Strategic Rocket Force, Ground Forces, Troops of National Air Defense, and Air Forces. The Navy also is a service of the Armed Forces. . . .''

3. During the 1930s, at the time these executions of Soviet citizens were taking place, few in the West realized their extent. Soviet writers make much of the manpower losses during the Civil War and World War II, but very rarely even mention that innocent people were killed in the 1930s.

4. See, for example, Harriet Fast Scott, "Russia's Growing Minorities Problem," *Air Force Magazine,* October 1979, p. 65.

5. As noted in Chapter 5, to stop the Novocherkassk riot of June 2, 1962, regular military units were sent from Rostov. Tanks entered the town square and an estimated fifty to eighty people were killed. Remaining individuals identified as having taken part in the riots were dispatched to Siberia. Aleksandr I. Solzhenitsyn, *The Gulag Archipelago,* Vol. 3. New York: Harper & Row, 1974, pp. 506–514.

6. P. Chirkin, *Granitsa Na Zamke* [The Border Under Lock and Key]. Moscow: Young Guards Publishing House, 1969. Also see A. T. Mar-

chenko, *60 Tysyach Pogranichnykh Kilometrov* [60,000 Kilometers of Border]. Moscow: Voyenizdat, 1972.

7. John Barron, *KGB — The Secret Work of Soviet Secret Agents.* New York: Bantam Books, 1974. For an account of the KGB organizational structure, see Chapter 3, pp. 85–95.

8. The KGB previously was "attached" *(pri)* to the Council of Ministers, U.S.S.R.

9. I. K. Yakovlev, "Vnutrenniye Voyska" [Internal Troops], *Sovetskaya Voyennaya Entsiklopediya,* 1976, Vol. 2, p. 165.

10. The authors noted Internal Troops in formation in side streets near the United States Embassy in Moscow during "demonstrations."

11. These schools appear to be much the same type as the "higher military schools" that provide education and training for cadets who are commissioned in military forces under the Ministry of Defense.

12. For a description of the training and other activities of Internal Troops, see *Prikazano Zastupit!* [Ordered to Protect!]. Moscow: Young Guards Publishing House, 1974.

13. N. A. Shelokov, *Sovetskaya Militsiya* [Soviet Militia]. Moscow: Znaniye Publishing House, 1971, p. 36.

14. In the early 1970s a series of eight pamphlets, *Library of the People's Guards,* were issued. Two of the titles are *Dobrovol'naya Narodnaya Druzhina Po Okhrane Obshchestvennogo Poryadka* [The Volunteer People's Guards in Guarding the Social Order] and *Rukovodstvo Narodnymi Druzhinami* [Leadership of the People's Guards]. These pamphlets, published in 1971, were issued by the Pravda Publishing House, Moscow.

15. For a discussion of the Soviet firefighting service, see G. A. Raschetin, *Na Strazhe ot Ognya* [On Protecting from Fires]. Moscow: Publishing House of Constructors, 1967.

16. F. Obukhov, "Profession of the Brave," *Voyennyye Znaniye,* No. 4, April 1968.

7
Civil Defense

In October 1972, only a few months after the signing of the SALT I treaty, the position of Chief of Civil Defense in the Soviet Union was raised to Deputy Minister of Defense level. Approximately a year later, in September 1973, the *Yezhegodnik, Bol'shoy Sovetskoy Entsiklopedii* listed *for the first time* the Troops of Civil Defense along with the Strategic Rocket Troops, Troops of National PVO, Ground Forces, Air Forces, Navy, Border Guards, and Internal Troops[1]. Very little is known in the West about the actual numbers and composition of these civil defense forces.

Civil defense in the Soviet Union is considered one aspect of military strategy. Soviet spokesmen attempt to describe it as a "peace-strengthening measure." For example:

> Soviet civil defense does not incite, does not promote, and does not provide impetus to war. Its substance is influenced in a decisive manner by the peaceful foreign policy of the socialist state. For this reason there is no basis for the "forecasts" of Western experts that a strengthening of Soviet civil defense will lead to greater "inflexibility" of Soviet foreign policy and even to serious aggravation of international tensions. Improvement of Soviet civil defense and an increase in its effectiveness constitutes one more major obstacle in the way of the unleashing of a new world war by the imperialists. Consequently, Soviet civil defense intensifies the peaceful actions taken by our state and strengthens international security as a whole. Herein lies one of the most important features of its sociopolitical essence.[2]

According to Soviet political-military spokesmen, any attempt in the capitalist world to create a civil defense system is doomed to failure. The primary obstacle is the private ownership of property. Civil defense, to be effective, demands the full utilization of a nation's resources. They assert that private ownership would preclude the use of land, buildings, transport, and other facilities necessary for a civil defense program.

In the Soviet Union "the strength and firmness of civil defense are the invincible strength and firmness of the socialist order." Overall direction to the program is given by the Party leadership.

> *Politics directly and indirectly* (through military doctrine and strategy) specifies the *objectives and missions of civil defense* and determines its place and role in achieving victory in war. For this reason, no matter what its organizational structure, the fundamental directions of its development and principles or operations are elaborated by the nation's political leaders.[3] [Emphasis added]

Soviet spokesmen, when discussing civil defense, stress that it is directed against an attack that the "imperialist aggressors" plan to launch against the peace-loving socialist states. They never acknowledge that a major reason for their massive civil defense program may be fear of an attack from another socialist nation — China. Nor do the Soviet writers suggest that, if an effective civil defense program is possible only in a socialist state, China might have a program as effective as their own.

In 1975, based partly on the glowing accounts Soviet spokesmen gave of their civil defense programs, Washington planners evidenced an interest in Soviet civil defense capabilities and how such programs might affect the strategic nuclear balance. Members of Soviet research institutes, particularly the Institute of the U.S.A. and Canada, apparently became concerned that Soviet civil defense programs might have an adverse impact upon arms control negotiations. Possibly recognizing that few in the United States read the Soviet press, some Soviet research institute members went out of their way to categorically deny that the U.S.S.R. had a civil defense program, or even Troops of Civil Defense. They deplored the way Soviet civil defense had been treated in the U.S. press.

In an apparent effort to camouflage attention to civil defense, Soviet authorities redesignated the Moscow Military School of Civil Defense, U.S.S.R., which had opened with some publicity in the late 1960s, as the Moscow Higher Command School of Road and Engineer Troops. Despite denials by members of Soviet research institutes concerning Soviet civil defense, there is no evidence in Soviet books, newspapers, and journals of any reduction in Soviet civil defense programs.[4] Possible exceptions to this are those Soviet journals written primarily for foreign readers, such as *USA,* the monthly journal of the Institute of the U.S.A. and Canada.

It is clear that in the event of a nuclear exchange a well-planned civil defense effort would have a major role in the success or failure of control measures. In fact, such an effort might be the determining factor.

Early Origins

As the Soviet people are accustomed to military districts, military commissariats, the KGB, and other systems that help to maintain control, they also are accustomed to civil defense. All of these organizations and concepts were developed in the early days of the Soviet state and utilized in World War II. All contribute elements to a control system of the magnitude essential for nuclear war conditions.

Decrees of the Soviet Council of Labor and Defense of 1927, which applied to civil defense, noted the need for civil defense personnel in factories, airports, rail and water transport installations, and major population centers. The entire U.S.S.R. was divided into civil defense regions. In cities, the local commanders of PVO (antiaircraft defense) often would be given responsibilities for civil defense.

Beginning with Stalin's first five-year plan in 1928, increased emphasis was placed on civil defenses against air attack and chemical weapons. Specific educational efforts were implemented in the western and southwestern parts of the Soviet Union, including Moscow, Leningrad, Kiev, Kharkov, and Baku. *Osoaviakhim* (Union of Societies of Cooperation in Defense and Aviation and Chemical Construction of the U.S.S.R.) attempted to get young people interested in defense matters, especially with respect to air and chemical defenses.

According to Soviet accounts, over 500,000 workers had been trained in anti-air and anti-gas defense measures by 1932. Several thousand shelters were constructed, and 3 million gas masks were manufactured. In the latter part of 1932 air defense was incorporated into a nationwide organization, MPVO (local anti-aircraft defense), under control of the NKVD. MPVO activities were closely integrated with the Red Army's Main Directorate of Anti-aircraft Defense (GUPVO) as well as with other bodies such as *Osoaviakhim,* the Soviet Red Cross, and the militia (civil police). All able-bodied men between 16 and 60 and women between 18 and 50 could be called up for compulsory service in MPVO, unless on active duty in a military organization.

Following a customary Soviet practice for generating enthusiasm, by 1935 norms were established for earning pins reading "Ready for Air and Chemical Defense," and annual competitions were initiated. By 1938 2,800,000 people were involved, and by 1940 there were 20,000 MPVO units. Soviet law at that time required that all new plants reflect a consideration of air defense measures in their construction.[5]

When Hitler launched his invasion of the Soviet Union there were 30 million gas masks in Soviet bomb shelters. However, the Soviets were by no means fully prepared. Factory workers engaged in civil defense had no guns with which to assist regular troops. When Moscow was expecting an air attack, preparations were slowed because Stalin had sent the Chief of his Air Defense Troops to prison. Active military commands had priority over MPVO units, and 12,000 civil defense workers were sent to help hold the front outside of Moscow.[6]

SNAVR (rescue and urgent disaster and restoration work) units were formed, and by the end of the war about 1 million workers were assigned to this organization. Mobile units of MPVO also were established.

In the postwar period increased attention was given to civil defense procedures. MPVO activities were organized into units on the union, republic, *kray,* and *oblast* levels. Services included warning, communications, preserving order, and safety. In 1957, the mandatory civil defense instruction program, which included not only defense against nuclear weapons but also against chemical and bacteriological agents,[7] was increased to 22 hours.

Khrushchev's announcement of a new military doctrine in 1960, which marked another stage in the development of the Soviet Armed Forces, led to increased attention to survival measures for the population. The basic tenet of the new doctrine was that any future world war into which nuclear powers were drawn would inevitably become a nuclear war. There would be no distinction between the front and rear areas; the entire nation would become a military theater. War would begin, according to Soviet spokesmen, with the "imperialists" launching a surprise nuclear strike against Soviet territory. There would be only a few minutes of warning time before the bombs would fall.

Assignment of Civil Defense to the Ministry of Defense

In 1960, MPVO was removed from the control of the Ministry of Internal Affairs and placed under the Ministry of Defense. In August 1961, at the time Khrushchev was increasing tension in Europe by building the Berlin Wall, MPVO was redesignated as Civil Defense, U.S.S.R. Marshal Vasiliy Chuykov, Commander-in-Chief of the Ground Forces, was given the additional title of Chief of Civil Defense. (The KGB at the time retained normal police, firefighting, and related responsibilities, and in emergencies their units would work with civil defense organs.)

Under the revised concept, civil defense was defined as:

A system of state defense measures, effected in time of peace and in war, with the aim of the defense of the population and objects of the national economy from nuclear, chemical, and bacteriological weapons, and also with the aim of conducting rescue and urgent damage-restoration work in "hotbeds" of mass destruction.[8]

The principal tasks to be undertaken under the new program were as follows:

- General instruction of the population about measures of defense against weapons of mass destruction;
- Preparation of individual and collective means of defense of the population;
- Creation of conditions ensuring the reliable work of necessary manufacturing, transport, communications, and energy supply in time of war;
- Preparation of civil defense forces;
- Timely warning of the population of the danger of enemy attack;
- Ensuring the defense of livestock, food, and water against weapons of mass destruction;

- Organization and conduct of rescue and urgent damage-restoration work in "hotbeds" of mass destruction.[9]

With respect to the tasks listed, Soviet spokesmen have emphasized that the primary purpose of civil defense is the defense of the population.

As changes in organizational structure and control of civil defense took place, there were corresponding changes in concepts. In the 1950s and early 1960s, major reliance was placed on a shelter program, similar to the plans that were being made in the United States at that time. Later, evacuation was deemed more feasible. There was a program for "green belts" of trees to be planted around the cities. Immediately beyond the green belt additional buildings could be constructed. The green belt would prevent fires from spreading, and the outer buildings would be placed sufficiently far from the center of the city to avoid destruction should the city come under nuclear attack.

The entire U.S.S.R. was divided into territorial areas for civil defense purposes, relying on the existing structure of the Soviet agencies in republics, *krays, oblasts,* cities, *rayons,* and village councils. All bodies of the economy and directing agencies, regardless of the ministry to which they belong, are organizationally part of the civil defense of the republic, *oblast,* region, and so on. All ministries and departments, enterprises, organizations, establishments, schools, *kolkhozes,* and *sovkhozes* were directed to adopt measures for protection from nuclear, chemical, and biological weapons. It was intended that Soviet civil defense activities be part of an overall structure in which the entire Soviet population would participate.

The responsibility for organizing civil defense measures in all civilian Soviet bodies was given to the executive committees of Workers' Soviets. Chairmen of the Workers' Soviets, who would be responsible for planning, training of the population, and building protective shelters, were designated as chiefs of civil defense for administrative bodies from *oblasts* down to villages. They were to be assisted by staffs and various services. As will be seen later, a great part of the work is done by the chiefs of staff for civil defense, who are military officers serving under the direction of the chairman.

Once civil defense control was placed under the Ministry of Defense, all ministries and departments were required to reexamine their programs. Shelter designs were restudied, and directives issued to the effect that all should have dual use. In time of peace, shelters were to be used as underground garages, theaters, restaurants, and the like. Such shelters were to have hermetically sealed doors and a filtered ventilation system. Gas masks and protective clothing were to be available, tested, and stored, with provisions made for their use in civil defense practices.

The new requirements brought about increases in personnel assigned to civil defense. Many regular officers, including a considerable number of generals, were assigned to key positions in the new civil defense structure. In particular, senior officers would serve as chiefs of staff of civil defense organizations in republics, *oblasts,* and lower administrative units. Some reserve and retired officers also appear to have been assigned full-time civil defense duties with nonmilitary groups.[10]

DOSAAF, the Red Cross, and the Red Crescent were charged with ensuring that all Soviet citizens receive civil defense training. Various individuals in specialized fields, such as engineers, technicians, medical workers, agricultural workers, were designated as instructors for particular civil defense measures. In 1966, the task of training the entire population in civil defense was given to the chiefs of civil defense in the various areas, with DOSAAF remaining an active participant in the training. This new program was in full force by 1967. A small booklet entitled *What Everyone Must Know*[11] was issued in 60 million copies and in all the languages used in the U.S.S.R. The press, radio, TV, and movies were directed to produce civil defense information that would reach the entire population.

Current Civil Defense Structure

At the 24th Party Congress in 1971, Party Secretary Brezhnev restated Lenin's dictum that "everything that the people have created must be reliably protected." More specific responsibilities were assigned for civil defense duties. The heads of ministries, departments, and economic enterprises were to be held accountable for

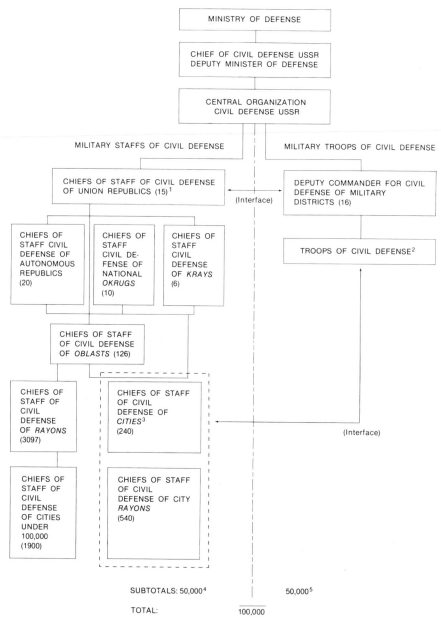

MINISTRY OF DEFENSE

CHIEF OF CIVIL DEFENSE USSR
DEPUTY MINISTER OF DEFENSE

CENTRAL ORGANIZATION
CIVIL DEFENSE USSR

MILITARY STAFFS OF CIVIL DEFENSE

MILITARY TROOPS OF CIVIL DEFENSE

CHIEFS OF STAFF OF CIVIL DEFENSE
OF UNION REPUBLICS (15)[1]

(Interface)

DEPUTY COMMANDER FOR CIVIL
DEFENSE OF MILITARY
DISTRICTS (16)

CHIEFS OF
STAFF CIVIL
DEFENSE OF
AUTONOMOUS
REPUBLICS
(20)

CHIEFS OF
STAFF
CIVIL DE-
FENSE OF
NATIONAL
OKRUGS
(10)

CHIEFS OF
STAFF
CIVIL
DEFENSE
OF KRAYS
(6)

TROOPS OF CIVIL DEFENSE[2]

CHIEFS OF STAFF
OF CIVIL DEFENSE
OF OBLASTS (126)

CHIEFS OF
STAFF OF
CIVIL
DEFENSE
OF RAYONS
(3097)

CHIEFS OF STAFF
OF CIVIL
DEFENSE OF
CITIES[3]
(240)

(Interface)

CHIEFS OF
STAFF OF
CIVIL
DEFENSE
OF CITIES
UNDER
100,000
(1900)

CHIEFS OF STAFF
OF CIVIL
DEFENSE OF CITY
RAYONS
(540)

SUBTOTALS: 50,000[4]   50,000[5]

TOTAL: 100,000

From a study by
Harriet Fast Scott and Christina F. Shelton.
1) Figures in parentheses reflect the numbers of union republics,
   military districts, republics, etc.
2) Detachment in every major Soviet city.
3) Cities larger than 100,000.
4) Military personnel on Civil Defense Staffs.
5) Est. number of Civil Defense troop units.

Figure 9. The Overall Structure of Soviet Civil Defense.

civil defense within their organizations. Party work in the staffs, services, and nonmilitary formations of civil defense establishments became the responsibility of the central committees of union republics, *krays, oblasts,* down to regional Party committees, and even to Party committees of economic enterprises.

As previously noted, in 1972 General-Colonel A. T. Altunin became the new Chief of Civil Defense and also a Deputy Minister of Defense. The following year the Troops of Civil Defense were described as follows:

> The Armed Forces of the U.S.S.R. consist of the Strategic Rocket Troops, Ground Forces, Air Forces, Troops of National Air Defense, Navy, *Civil Defense,* Border, and Internal Troops.[12] [Emphasis added]

The civil defense structure took into account the need for various functions that must be performed and how they should be carried out. For example:

- Communication service — to provide warning to the proper authorities and the people of the danger of enemy attack through the civil defense warning system. The chief of communications for the area is to work with civil defense authorities to provide the necessary network.
- Medical services — under the overall direction of civil defense personnel, hospitalization, evacuation, anti-epidemic and sanitary work will be carried out, using local health and medical facilities.
- Service and maintaining civil order — to control the population and ensure that all decrees of the Executive Committee of the Council of Workers' Deputies that pertain to civil defense have been carried out at installations and factories, and by the people. This service is to control panic and also guard state property and personal property of citizens, and isolate centers of destruction or of contamination. The overall responsibility for ensuring order will be that of the chief of the militia directorate. (In the event martial law is declared, the responsibility for maintaining order would be the military

commander's. He would use the facilities of the organized militia and whatever other means might be needed.)

- Firefighting service — to reduce the danger of fires in factories, homes, woods, or any area, and to conduct rescue and firefighting work caused by an enemy attack or natural calamities. This would be accomplished through the municipal fire department.

- Engineering service — to provide access routes through rubble, demolition of unstable buildings, and moving rubble in order that people may be rescued. In time of peace, the municipal engineering service is concerned with the problem of building shelters. In time of war, the engineering service for civil defense is provided by municipal construction agencies.

- Animal and plant life protection service — provided by agricultural and veterinary directorates, experimental stations, tree planting trusts, and other establishments.

- Transport service — provided by transportation directorates, using all means of transportation available. A primary task is to provide for the transportation of evacuated and dispersed workers and employees into the outer areas.

- Power service — provided by the Department of Power Supply, to ensure uninterrupted supply of energy to designated industrial plants and to ensure proper procedures during blackouts.

- Provisions and supplies service — organized in the directorate of commerce and food supplies. Responsible for planning and conducting measures to protect food products, supplies of consumable raw materials, and industrial commodities. It also secures food products and other essential products for the injured and evacuated population, and organizes the feeding of personnel and of the population working at centers of destruction.

- Technical service — provides repair and maintenance of vehicles and other equipment. Also responsible for the evacuation of equipment when required.

- Material-technical supply service — furnishes construction materials, decontamination and washing equipment, space equipment, and automobile parts.[13]

The Troops of Civil Defense

It is not known when the Troops of Civil Defense were established, and very little is known about their size. As early as 1965 a Soviet military journal carried a photograph with the caption, "Civil Defense Troops"; more extensive research would likely find earlier references to such troops. Since the early 1970s references to Civil Defense Troops and photographs of their activities have appeared with considerable frequency in the Soviet military and political-military press.

The Moscow Military School of Civil Defense opened in March 1967. Students entered between the ages of 18 and 22, which is customary for military personnel attending such schools. This was to be a three-year school, and its graduates received a commission and a diploma, not a degree as at the higher military schools. The course was divided into two specialty areas, and a student could become either a mechanic-technician or a radio-technician. The first class graduated in two years; succeeding classes were to go the full three years.[14] As previously noted, in the mid-1970s this school "went underground," apparently due to the problem Soviet spokesmen had on the one hand of trying to extol the virtues of the school and a civil defense program to Soviet citizens while on the other hand denying its existence to the West.

Troops of civil defense are assigned to the military districts and probably collocated with various units; contingents are stationed in cities. Each military district headquarters has a deputy commander for civil defense, usually an officer with the rank of general-major. (See Figure 9.)

Units of the Troops of Civil Defense are manned by the customary Soviet two-year military call-ups, who afterward are "transferred into the reserves." It would seem probable that those who have served in the Troops of Civil Defense while on active duty will also have a mobilization assignment in this same force.

The "Civilian" Civil Defense Structure

The "civilian" civil defense structure is the nationwide apparatus concerned with the protection of the population as a whole and the economy, and post-atomic recovery. The activities of the "civilian" side of civil defense are controlled by the Chief of Civil Defense, who is also a Deputy Minister of Defense.

Heads of ministries, departments, and economic enterprises are responsible for civil defense in their specific organizations. Much of the actual civil defense planning, however, is the job of the "chiefs of staff" for civil defense, who are assigned to the various republics, autonomous republics, *oblasts,* and cities of 100,000 population and over. (It is possible that smaller cities have "chiefs of staff" for civil defense, although data are lacking.) The military chief of staff also provides a connecting link to the Ministry of Defense.

All the chiefs of staff for civil defense serving in the republics appear to be at least general-majors, and two general-lieutenants have been identified in these positions. All have sizeable staffs. For example, the chief of staff for civil defense in the RSFSR is a general-lieutenant, with general-majors for staff representatives and for deputy chief of staff for political units. A colonel serves as deputy chief of staff for combat training. (It must be kept in mind that this is merely the identified portion of the staff of the chief of staff for civil defense, and is not associated with the military district.)

The autonomous republics in the RSFSR have colonels in the position of chief of staff for civil defense. The same rank structure applies to national *okrugs* (districts), *krays,* and *oblasts.* Officers in the rank of lieutenant colonel have been identified as the deputy chiefs of staff for civil defense in *oblasts.*

The ranks of the chiefs of staff of civil defense assigned to cities vary, apparently with the size and importance of a city. The city of Moscow has a general–major in this capacity, while Odessa, population 892,000, has a colonel. Perm, population 850,000, and Komsomolsk-na-Amur, population 218,000, have lieutenant–colonels in the position. On the other hand, Orsha, population 101,000, has a colonel assigned.[15]

It must be stressed that the names and ranks of only a small fraction of the chiefs of staff of civil defense at various levels have been identified. However, there is every reason to believe that the positions are filled throughout the entire U.S.S.R. at all the administrative levels with men of the approximate ranks indicated.

Based on the number of administrative units — republics, autonomous republics, national *okrugs, krays, oblasts, rayons,* and cities — the number of senior officers assigned to civil defense duties appears approximately as follows: 100 generals, 400 colonels, 5,500 lieutenant colonels and majors, for a total of 6,000 officers ranked major and above. This number by no means includes the full military complement. As noted, the larger administrative units have senior officers as deputy chiefs of staff, as deputy chiefs of staff for political units, and so on. When considering all associated military personnel who seemingly would serve the offices of the chiefs of staff for civil defense, it is unlikely that this figure is less than 50,000.

The extensive military element on the civilian side of civil defense facilitates coordination with civil defense troops assigned to the military districts and at the same time provides a direct chain to the Ministry of Defense. Interface also could readily be provided between the troops of civil defense stationed in or near cities and the chief of staff for civil defense in the city itself.

Preparation of the Population

The first and primary task of Soviet civil defense is protection of the population, and a necessary element of protection is preparation. Preparation includes providing for the people not only shelters, but also individual protective measures, such as gas masks, protective clothing, and medical kits.

The method used for shelters has varied in the past according to the type of weapons that might be used by an attacker as well as the level and expected type of attack. This was explained in 1975, as follows:

> Here it must be recalled that in the not distant past the main method of protecting the population was considered to be evacuation and dispersion.
>
> Now, when further development and improvement of the nuclear rocket weapon and strategic aviation have taken place, the aggressor in the event of unleashing war might make an attempt to carry out a preemptive nuclear rocket strike. Such a variant for unleashing war might be tempting for the imperialists. In these conditions the time for

protective measures of civil defense might be very limited, especially the time needed to carry out dispersal and evacuation.

Consequently, today the plan to shelter the population in protective structures has been placed in the forefront as the most reliable method of preserving people's lives from nuclear rocket weapons. It is obvious that if such protection is assured then a person will not be threatened with destruction by other kinds of weapons.[16]

This shift from evacuation and dispersion to a return to a greater reliance on shelters suggests a Soviet reappraisal of the primary threat. Such a reappraisal may have taken place shortly after the U.S. Secretary of Defense James Schlesinger's announcement in January 1974 of the possibility of limited nuclear options, or selective strikes. The Soviet leadership might have realized that it would not be the intent of the United States simply to attack the population, but to strike primary military targets. Another possibility might have been, perhaps allied with the first, that shelters would be the better means of protecting the population in the event of a limited nuclear strike by China.

Subways in the larger Soviet cities provide excellent shelters for hundreds of thousands of people, and long-range Soviet planning calls for subways in all cities with populations over one million. Systems built thus far have massive blast doors and are deep, and these alone could provide shelter for a considerable percentage of the people in major population centers.

In the event of an attack, the city might already be under martial law, which would place all resources under control of a military commander. He might be the chief of staff for civil defense in a particular city or a representative of the commander of the military district in which the city is located. Based on the provisions of military legislation that apply to martial law, there seems to be no reason why the military commander could not be an officer in the Internal Troops or even the KGB general in the area. In any event, the provisions of martial law require a military figure to take command. All individuals not assigned other military duties could be mobilized for civil defense tasks.

Soviet civil defense planning is based primarily on one's place of work or school. Each factory or establishment is required to have shelters for its personnel as well as an evacuation plan (and, if part of an essential industry, a mobilization plan). Civil defense drills are required, and workers are divided, at least on paper, into teams that are responsible for certain civil defense measures. Until the factory manager was made responsible for civil defense training of personnel in his plant, civil defense drills were reportedly half-hearted affairs. It is difficult to determine where preparation of the population ends and preparation of the economy begins.

Preparation of the Economy

In the event of a protracted nuclear war, the side that can keep its economy functioning after the initial nuclear exchange would be the one more likely to regain the strategic initiative. Soviet military strategists state that even in a short war the winning side will require a productive capability in order to consolidate its victory. This requires the maintenance of some industry, essential transportation and communications, and an agricultural yield sufficient to feed the nation. Prior to or immediately after the beginning of a nuclear war, the management and direction of the Soviet national economy likely would be closely integrated with the Soviet *Tyl,* under the direction of GKO. This would be effected, as necessary, through the military commander, should the particular area be under martial law.

When discussing the economic aspect of nuclear warfare, Soviet theorists note that

> . . . a significant index of economic preparedness, along with the general level of economic development, is the structure of the economy. Nowadays fundamental importance has been acquired by the preferential development of such branches of industry as atomic, rocket, aviation, radio engineering, and chemical.[17]

There are no openly published data in the Soviet Union to compare the "preferential development" of the industries cited above with industrial development in other sectors. However, Soviet actual production of advanced weapons systems suggests that such preferential treatment has been accorded.

Soviet military planners recommend that essential industries be duplicated to provide for actual nuclear war conditions. It is impossible to determine to what degree this has been accomplished.

When considering the economic development of the U.S.S.R. as a whole, it is unlikely this has been achieved except possibly in a few very critical areas.

Attempts to provide duplicate production facilities appear to be associated with the division of the Soviet Union into eighteen "economic zones." According to some Soviet spokesmen, the division into economic zones is based "more on the social division of labor than on the prevailing natural or other conditions." Marshal Grechko, when outlining the directives of the 24th Party Congress to the Soviet Armed Forces, spoke specifically about the "scattered placement" of Soviet productive forces. Such dispersal "makes our industry less vulnerable in the event that imperialism unleashes a nuclear missile war."[18] The United States, because of its concentration of industry, is some three times as vulnerable to nuclear attack as the Soviet Union, according to Marshal Grechko.

Food would be a critical problem for any nation undergoing a nuclear attack, and also during recovery. It has been reported that the Soviet Union has emergency grain storage centers. If these actually do exist, they are part of the "untouchable reserves" referred to occasionally in Soviet writings.[19] However, despite any amount of food that might be stored, large areas of the Soviet Union would have critical shortages following a nuclear attack of any magnitude. Little of the huge land area east of the Urals is good for agriculture, and in the early days of World War II, Soviet agricultural output decreased by 38 percent. This loss was only partly offset by huge food shipments from the United States and other Western nations.

Soviet mobilization plans include the call-up of most of the able-bodied workers in agriculture, as well as a great part of the agricultural machinery — tractors, trucks, bulldozers, and similar equipment. Since food production already is marginal, it is unlikely that anything approaching even current agricultural efforts could be maintained except under conditions of a very limited attack.

It is impossible to determine with any degree of certainty the extent to which Soviet planners actually have prepared the economy for nuclear war and how well it might function at any level of attack. A number of Soviet cities with populations over one million — Gorky, Chelyabinsk, and Sverdlovsk, for example —

are closed to foreigners. Even in so-called open areas, such as the Moscow *oblast,* many areas are in fact closed. With respect to specific industrial plants, members of the Moscow diplomatic community occasionally are taken through a vodka or candy plant, but seldom to any industry where even ordinary consumer goods are produced. A few foreign visitors, or individuals in industries who have something the Soviets wish to buy, may be given slightly more access. But there are few actual firm data on Soviet productive capabilities of essential goods, possible duplication of key military industries, and the like. Even production outputs of civilian goods are often classified.

In all probability, Soviet achievements in preparing the economy for the possibility of a nuclear war are far short of goals, and in some areas it is most likely that no progress whatever has been made. On the other hand, it should be safe to assume that actual work has been accomplished in a few critical areas.

Psychological Preparation of the Population

The purpose of civil defense training is to provide citizens with the knowledge of how to protect themselves and of what means of protection might be available. Moral-political preparation, or psychological preparation, is "interrelated and supplementary" to civil defense. Moral-political preparation extends throughout the Armed Forces and the entire population. Dozens of books and hundreds of articles on the subject are published each year. The foreword to *Military Psychology,* a Soviet textbook, states that "great attention is given to the psychological preparation of Soviet soldiers for combat actions in conditions of nuclear-rocket war."[20]

Within recent years, Soviet spokesmen — writing primarily in Soviet journals that are known to be studied in the West — have concentrated on "the myth of the Soviet threat." Soviet visitors to the United States, as well as Soviet hosts of visiting Americans in Moscow, deny that activities such as civil defense and psychological preparation of the population exist. *Intourist* guides have taken up the same theme. Soviet spokesmen at all levels make a concentrated effort to conceal evidences of a military presence in the country.

The "moral-political preparation" of the population continues as the theme of a certain segment of Soviet writings, both civilian and military. Evidences of this can be found in cities outside of the Moscow–Leningrad–Kiev *Intourist* circuit. The concept is well explained in the excerpt below. What is said is applicable both in preparing the Soviet people for the invasion of another nation, such as Czechoslovakia or Afghanistan, and the possibility of a nuclear war.

The moral-political preparation of the population is of decisive importance under the present-day conditions, since the use of weapons of mass destruction in war imposes exceptionally high, previously unheard-of demands on the political morale of the population.

The political-moral preparation of the Soviet people for war consists mainly in educating them in the spirit of Soviet patriotism, love of country and the Communist Party, and teaching them to be ready to suffer any hardships of war for the purpose of achieving victory.

The Soviet people are brought up on the ideas of defending their country and the achievements of the socialist revolution, the conviction of the superiority of the socialist system over the capitalist system, and confidence in the structure of the communist society . . . .

Therefore, one of the tasks involved in educating the populace is to decisively unmask the reactionary nature of American politics and propaganda, which strive to present "the American way of life" in a rosy light, to show present-day capitalism as "democratic," peaceful, and humane, to conceal the aggressive nature of its politics, and to present preparations for unleashing war as defensive measures.

It is very important to convince the people of the justice of those goals which the Soviet Union and the entire socialist camp will pursue in a war. The people must be deeply convinced of the indestructible unity of the countries of the socialist camp, of the wise leadership of the Communist and Workers' parties, of the economic might of the Soviet Union.

It is necessary to instill in the people a belief in the might of our Armed Forces and love for them, as well as a belief in the strength of the fighting union of the armed forces of the socialist countries . . . .

As a result of socialist transformations and extensive educational work carried out by the Communist party and the Soviet government, there has been formed and is now developing in our country a new Soviet man, an active builder of communism, a fervent patriot of his country, ardent champion of a new life, ready to undergo any sacrifices in the name of freedom and independence of his country, capable of overcoming any difficulties on the path to victory. This new man, who possesses a high level of morale and technical culture, will, in the event of war, be a decisive factor in our victory.[21]

The Soviet leadership is not content merely with attempts to instill a strong sense of patriotism in the population. As shown above, an active hatred of the "class enemy," generally portrayed as the United States, is part of Soviet ideological indoctrination. The ideological struggle, as Marshal L. I. Brezhnev stressed in the post-SALT I period, is continued with increased vigor during periods of detente. For example, on August 2, 1979, a speaker of the Znaniye Society addressed a group in Sevastopol on "American Imperialism: The Bulwark of World Reaction." This was his 1,500th lecture on the subject. The ideological struggle, according to Soviet pronouncements, is an essential part of peaceful coexistence and is waged by all of the news media. Those who have never read Soviet newspapers, journals, or books, or who have never listened to Soviet radio or watched Soviet television, may find it difficult to visualize the effort that goes into this ideological conditioning. In part, this is psychological preparation for the possibility of war, either nuclear or conventional.

Indoctrination of Soviet Youth

In 1978, a Britisher who had just completed a trip on the Trans-Siberian Railroad from Moscow to Nakhodka remarked how he was reminded of Hitler's Germany of the late 1930s. Never since that time had he seen so much attention given to the militarization of youth. He found it strange that so little of this had been dealt with in the British press.[22]

What the Englishman found in 1978 was considerably different from the situation of the early 1960s. During the so-called "cold war" period of Nikita Khrushchev it was difficult to find toys of a military nature in Soviet stores of any type. There was no apparent attempt to indoctrinate the very young in the glory of military forces. Soviet television programs directed at pre-teen youth did not emphasize violence.

By 1970 a marked change had taken place. Toy guns, missiles, tanks, military aircraft, and the like were prominently displayed in children's toy stores. A 1972 article in *Morskoy Sbornik* stated that "bringing up a future soldier begins, if you please, with childhood."[23] In 1973, an article in *Red Star* stated that "people are not born soldiers, they become soldiers." The author urged that training and indoctrination for military service should begin "at the time of the first signs of maturity, during the time of adolescent dreams."[24] In the very first grades of school, Soviet teachers are directed to instill in each child a recognition of the needs of defense and "a readiness and ability to defend the homeland with a gun in hand."[25] An expensively illustrated book, published in 300,000 copies, described how a 12-year-old boy became the commandant of a group of new settlers and fought off an invader.[26]

Children between 11 and 15 years of age are encouraged to participate in *Zarnitsa,* a "military-sport" event started in 1967 for both boys and girls. The Pioneer Handbook, *Tovarishch* [Comrade], describes the games: the battalion is the basic unit, lower units are detachments, which have 3–4 scouts, 2–3 communications personnel, 7–12 riflemen, 2 medical corps men, 2 cooks, and an editor for the battalion combat journal. Approximately 1 million youths each year participate in these games.[27]

The *Zarnitsa* games proved so successful that in 1972 *Orlenok* was started, a game series for young people between 16 and 18. Civil defense exercises are played out, and participants fire small-caliber guns and throw hand grenades. Winning teams are brought into major Soviet cities, such as Moscow and Leningrad, and treated with honors.[28]

It might be difficult to get young people in the United States to participate in games such as *Orlenok.* But to the Soviet youths outside of the major *Intourist* centers, such as Moscow, Leningrad, Kiev, Tbilisi, and a few other cities where foreigners are allowed to visit, life is grim. There is little entertainment of the type Western youths are accustomed to; even cities of 100,000 or more may not have hard-surface roads linking them with other populated areas. Participating in the *Zarnitsa* and *Orlenok* is probably much more exciting to Soviet youths than one would at first think.

The basic purpose of these military–sports games, as their names imply, is to better prepare the populace for defense; simulated nuclear attacks are a regular part of the activities. This is part of the psychological preparation of the population for nuclear war.

DOSAAF (Volunteer Society for Cooperation with the Army, Aviation, and the Fleet)

In the event of a nuclear war, the discipline and training of Soviet youth could provide a significant advantage to the Soviet Union. After they reach the age of 14 a number of official Soviet agencies support their military indoctrination and some military training. The largest and most important of these is DOSAAF.

DOSAAF is a "defense-patriotic organization whose purpose is active cooperation for strengthening the military capability of the country and for preparing workers for the defense of the socialist fatherland."[29] It has been in existence since 1951, when individual youth organizations for cooperation with the Soviet Ground Forces, Navy, and Air Forces were combined into the present structure. DOSAAF clubs can be found in cities and towns throughout the entire Soviet Union. They provide facilities for many sports and other recreation, all of which are directed toward improving the ability of the participants to perform military duties. In 1967, the New Universal Military Service Law specifically assigned certain responsibilities to DOSAAF for pre-induction training.[30] Since that time a number of schools for military training have been started, with part of the staffs being regular active duty officers. DOSAAF is commanded by a general, admiral, or marshal on active duty, with numerous other active duty officers assigned.

DOSAAF has 341,000 primary organizations and 95 million members.[31] It has trained 25 million "sportsmen" in "military-technical types of sports." The organization publishes a wide variety of journals and books, as well as the newspaper *Soviet Patriot*. Its official journal, *Military Knowledge,* also is the civil defense journal.

By itself, DOSAAF would not be a major factor in assisting the control structure in the event of a nuclear war. But along with other Soviet organizations, such as the *Komsomol* and the military commissariat, it is yet another part in the total control mechanism. DOSAAF leaders and instructors could be quickly mobilized and possess the necessary background for further civil defense work. The military-sports games are designed to instill confidence in the people. Even though such training probably is never up to the claims of the Soviet leaders, it does exist.

Possible Impact of Civil Defense

Whether or not a Soviet civil defense program would ensure the survival of the Soviet population in the event of an all-out nuclear war is a much debated subject in the West. In a limited nuclear exchange, however, in which only a small number of weapons were used, civil defense training, to include "moral-political preparation," could be the means that keeps the population functioning.

Soviet military psychology emphasizes the need to develop conditioned reflexes in response to certain situations. In time of stress an individual's reactions will depend on his training and indoctrination, or lack thereof. Blind panic on the part of the population can be lessened if people have been conditioned and prepared for the possibility of a nuclear war.

It is often argued that Soviet citizens do not take civil defense seriously. This should be expected. Anyone who has ever seen a Soviet citizen at work would be very much surprised if he or she were to show any interest in civil defense or in any other government-imposed program. A Soviet clerk completely indifferent to helping any customer in a store would be equally indifferent to a civil defense exercise. The Communist Party leadership has a civil defense program headed by a Deputy Minister of Defense. He has the means to enforce his program, should that be necessary.

It should be pointed out that many Soviet citizens hardly ever take their "moral-political preparation" seriously. Comments made by a Soviet crowd during a military parade, or as Pioneer youths march by, attest to the fact that a certain percentage of the population either regard the training with disgust, or as a joke. The majority, however, take it as something that must be endured.

The Soviet civil defense program alone is not intended to be the sole means of population control in nuclear war conditions. In those areas where martial law has been declared it would be but one very important aspect of the total Soviet control program, under the direction of the Party and the military command.

NOTES

1. *Yezhegodnik, 1973, Bol'shoy Sovetskoy Entsiklopedii* [Yearbook, 1973, of the Great Soviet Encyclopedia]. Moscow: Soviet Encyclopedia Publishing House, 1973, p. 68.
2. A. S. Milovidov, *Filosofskoye Naslediye V. I. Lenina i Problemy Sovremennoy Voyny* [The Philosophical Heritage of V. I. Lenin and Problems of Contemporary War]. Moscow: Voyenizdat, 1972, p. 68.
3. Ibid., p. 336.
4. This is based on a continuing analysis of fifteen Soviet journals and three newspapers: *Pravda, Krasnaya Zvezda,* and *Sovetskiy Patriot.*
5. K. G. Kotlukov et al., *Grazhdanskaya Oborona Vchera i Sevodnya* [Civil Defense Yesterday and Today]. Moscow: Atomizdat, 1975.
6. N. Khrushchev, *Khrushchev Remembers,* edited by E. Crankshaw. Boston: Little, Brown & Company, 1970, p. 68.
7. K. G. Kotlukov, *Ot MPVO — K Grazhdanskoy Oboronye* [From MPVO to Civil Defense]. Moscow: Atomizdat, 1969, p. 64.
8. Ibid., pp. 64–65.
9. Ibid., p. 65.
10. For identification of Soviet officers in civil defense positions, see Harriet Fast Scott and Christina F. Shelton, *A Preliminary Net Assessment of the Manpower Involved in the US/U.S.S.R. Civil Defense Programs,* General Electric–TEMPO Center for Advanced Studies, Washington, D.C. GE-76-TMP-54A, November 1, 1976, pp. B-1 and C-5.
11. G. P. Isakov, *Eto Dolzhen Znat' Kazhdyy* [What Everyone Must Know]. Moscow: DOSAAF, 1969. Later the title of the basic booklet was changed to *Eto Dolzhen Znat' i Umet' Kazhdyy* [What Everyone Must Know and be Able to Do], and published both by DOSAAF and Voyenizdat. The number of copies published was not disclosed.
12. *Yezhegodnik, 1973,* p. 68.
13. Harriet Fast Scott and Christina F. Shelton, op. cit., pp. C-1 to C-14.
14. O. P. Nikolayev, "The Competition Was Strong," *Voyennyye Znaniye,* April 1968, p. 25.
15. Harriet Fast Scott and Christina F. Shelton, op. cit., pp. C-1 to C-14.

16. K. G. Kotlukov et al., *Grazhdanskaya Oborona Vchera i Sevod-nya,* op. cit., p. 90.

17. A. S. Zheltov, *Metodologicheskiye Problemy Voyennoy Teorii i Praktiki* [Methodological Problems of Military Theory and Practice]. Moscow: Voyenizdat, 1969, p. 128.

18. A. A. Grechko, *Na Strazhe Mira i Stroitel'stva Kommunizma* [On Guard Over the Peace and the Building of Communism]. Moscow: Voyenizdat, 1971, p. 38.

19. V. K. Vysotskiy, *Tyl Sovetskoy Armii,* op. cit., pp. 66–67.

20. M. I. Dyachenko and N. F. Fedenko, *Voyennaya Psikhologiya* [Military Psychology]. Moscow: Voyenizdat, 1967, p. 2.

21. V. D. Sokolovskiy, *Soviet Military Strategy,* Third Edition, op. cit., p. 329.

22. Conversation with six British doctors during a 1978 trip by the authors on the Trans-Siberian Railway.

23. G. Bardashchuk, "Commissioned as an Officer," *Morskoy Sbornik* [Naval Collections], September 1972, p. 69.

24. N. Nikol'skiy, "They are Becoming Soldiers," *Krasnaya Zvezda,* March 22, 1973.

25. O. Volodin, "Developing the Defenders of the Homeland," *Narodnoye Obrazovaniye* [Popular Education], February 1972, p. 30.

26. A. Duginets, *Dvenadtsatiletniy General* [The Twelve-Year-Old General]. Moscow: Little Child's Publishing House, 1970.

27. L. Yakovleva, *Tovarishch* [Comrade]. Moscow: Young Guards Publishing House, 1972, pp. 251–252. Also see V. Nikolayev, "Zarnitsa — Schools of Courage," *Voyennyye Znaniya* [Military Knowledge], May 1974, p. 19.

28. L. Pestrev, "It is Not a Vacation in 'Orlenok'," *Voyennyye Znaniya,* April 4, 1975.

29. *Bol'shaya Sovetskaya Entsiklopediya,* op. cit., Vol. 8, p. 465.

30. M. A. Belikov et al., editors, *Uchebnoye Posobiye Po Nachal- 'noy Voyennoy Podgotovke* [Textbook for Beginning Military Training]. Moscow: Voyenizdat, 1975, p. 33.

31. *Yezhegodnik, 1981, Bol'shoy Sovetskoy Entsiklopedii* [Yearbook, 1981, of the Great Soviet Encyclopedia]. Moscow: Soviet Encyclopedia Publishing House, 1981, p. 23.

8
Post-Attack Recovery

The Soviet control system, developed over a period of six decades, has withstood severe tests. In preparation for the possibility of a future war, legal measures — such as martial law, wartime laws, rights of requisition, and other statutes — are currently used to justify and to explain in advance how control would be effected in a wartime situation. Specific attention is given to the restoration of the economy following destruction caused by military actions.

Given these advance preparations and the effectiveness demonstrated by the Soviet control structure in the past, it is possible that under certain conditions the Soviet Communist Party system might survive a nuclear exchange and accomplish post-attack recovery. The backward state of the Soviet economy might make economic recovery more rapid than could be accomplished in the United States. In addition, the Soviet Union has huge reserves of natural resources so that few raw materials would need to be imported from abroad. Equally important, the majority of the Soviet population experienced or participated in the postwar recovery efforts following World War II.

The damage that a nation might suffer as a result of nuclear strikes, and the difficulty of restoration of the economy and societal organizations may defy analysis. But some indication of how recovery might be approached in the Soviet Union can be obtained from an examination of existing Soviet organizations that might play a role in restoration, current Soviet accounts of the lessons of World War II, and the nature of the Soviet economic structure.

SNAVR (Rescue and Urgent Disaster and Restoration Work)

In the immediate post-attack period, SNAVR would have the task of locating and marking areas of contamination; localizing and extinguishing fires; giving first aid and evacuating the injured; removing the population from areas threatened by flooding; disinfecting people; decontaminating clothing, transport, equipment, buildings, and related facilities; and protecting livestock and plant life.

Such missions would be carried out by all available personnel, including troop units, nonmilitary formations, civil defense establishments, and other organizations according to civil defense plans. Direction would come from Party officials through the military command responsible for enforcing martial law, if designated for the area.[1]

The Pattern from World War II

The post-attack recovery phase would be significantly influenced by the experiences and perceived lessons of World War II, in relation to present circumstances. Accounts of how the Soviet Union survived that war play a dominant role in the education, training, and indoctrination of all Soviet citizens. Numerous books, such as *The Soviet Tyl in the Great Patriotic War* (discussed in Chapter 3), help instill "moral-patriotic" qualities in the Soviet populace as well as provide lessons applicable to any future conflict.

Leonid Brezhnev's 1978 monograph, *Rebirth,* describes the rebuilding of the Dnieper Hydroelectric Power Station in the immediate post-World War II period, a responsibility assigned him by the Central Committee. He stressed methods used in the restoration of the economy and in civil control in a devastated area. This monograph, along with two others by Brezhnev, won the Lenin Prize for the year and was the topic at Party meetings throughout the nation, high-level military conferences, and dozens of other activities associated with moral-political indoctrination. The attention given to this work was not simply due to its historical value. Indeed, an apparent purpose was to convince the population that a nation could be rebuilt following a war and occupation by an enemy. The lessons learned were applicable to the present and the future.

According to Brezhnev, Hitler had been told that 25 years would be needed to restore what had been destroyed. "The U.S. imperialists wanted to believe the most gloomy of forecasts because by that time they had sharply changed their attitude toward the U.S.S.R., their ally in the anti-Hitler coalition." The United States "denied us turbines and generators," and therefore Soviet workers had to produce all of the needed equipment, which turned out to be "more reliable and more powerful than their American counterparts." The "reborn" power station produced its first electricity early in the spring of 1947, achieving "the impossible by restoring this most complex branch of industry in a single year."[2]

Brezhnev emphasized that the Communist Party was responsible for the successful completion of the task. Restoration of the power station "was recognized as a classical model of the concentration of forces and means on decisive sectors of the nationwide construction campaign."[3] He claimed that the experience has been used since at various places, such as for the construction of the Kama automobile works. (No mention was made of the fact that this plant was designed and constructed by an American firm.) At the same time in the nearby city there were no street lights, telephones, or city transport. "Even armed bands would put in an appearance, and shots could sometimes be heard at night."[4] (One of Brezhnev's first actions was to raise the strength and prestige of the militia.)

"There as yet existed no science of the restoration of destroyed factories and the like, or textbooks to tell us how a structure that had been razed to the ground or blown up could be raised from the ashes." Brezhnev stated that risks had to be taken and everything had to be done as if for the first time. The short deadline given to place the plant into operation had to be shortened even more because of the "onset of the cold war"[5] Construction work of such magnitude could not have been accomplished without "active and effective help from the Central Committee of the CPSU (B) and the Council of Ministers of the U.S.S.R."[6]

Brezhnev's version of the "rebirth" following World War II's destruction is but one of the hundreds of accounts about that war being published in the Soviet Union today. They are not written to provide more accurate and complete data about that war, but to indoctrinate the population in the necessity of Party control and to assert that the Soviet Union will survive any future conflict.

Basic Survival

From accounts and practices of World War II, as well as from observations of the present Soviet state, some factors in any possible future war can be determined with reasonable certainty. In seriously damaged areas, martial law probably would be declared. Either Internal Troops or troops from the military districts would maintain order under the direction of local Party representatives. Local Councils of Defense would have been established, whose edicts would carry the force of law.

Present inefficiencies of Soviet production might actually assist in restoring some industries in rural areas after a nuclear strike. Even at present, spare parts for Soviet equipment and machinery, from automobiles to tractors, are often unobtainable. *Kolkhozes* maintain their own blacksmith shops where spare parts for farm equipment are made. Ancient cars are often kept running by hand-made parts. Factories that do produce basic items generally are less complex than those in the United States and probably would be easier to get back in operation.

Providing shelters for the populace would be an initial task in the post-attack recovery period. The present nature of Soviet society and economy may make the task less difficult than is generally thought. Today, from Moscow to Vladivostok, the majority of the population in the latitude of the Trans-Siberian Railway live in log houses. These houses are seen not only in villages and small towns, but also on the outskirts of large cities. Although electricity is supplied, they seldom have central heating or indoor plumbing.[7] Most villages could be rebuilt with virtually nothing supplied from factories. The primary requirement would be log transport to the necessary areas. In areas where wood is scarce the natives live in rather primitive shelters built of local materials.

Since the early 1970s, tens of thousands of "dachas" (summer homes) have been constructed on the outskirts of Soviet cities. These are located between 10 and 40 kilometers from the city center, on small plots of ground where vegetables are grown. A few of the houses are two-story, and although they are not heated, these houses would serve as emergency shelters for people fleeing the city.

Rural life in the Soviet Union is on a much more basic level than in the United States. People are used to "doing without" and enduring hardships. They can and often do build their own homes and grow their own food. In fact, a considerable part of total Soviet food production can be attributed to small, individual plots tended by peasants and city workers. When expensive, complicated farm machinery breaks down, as it frequently does, the people can be seen harvesting grain or putting in their crops as their ancestors did during the reign of Peter the Great.

Restoration of Transportation and Communications

Transportation and communications are essential to the Soviet control structure. How rapidly they could be restored following a nuclear exchange would be a determining factor in the Soviet ability to effect post-atomic recovery.

Railroads

The Soviet Union of the early 1980s, having no highway system linking the western and eastern regions of the nation, is as dependent upon its railroad system as was the United States at the beginning of the century. The railroads employ almost 1-1/2 million workers, a semimilitarized force with a rank structure and even rank insignia. Internal Troops are sometimes assigned to work directly with railway officials to provide security. Should a major war occur, the railroads would be placed under martial law just as during World War II — without any advance notice or disruption of rail operations.

Several problems would exist in restoring rail operations following nuclear strikes. Many of the major Soviet lines are electrified, and some time would be required to restore electrical facilities. Other engines require diesel fuel, which might be difficult to obtain if oil shipments were interrupted or oil facilities destroyed.

For any possible emergency, the Soviets store hundreds of coal-burning locomotives, which can be seen by the dozens along the Trans-Siberian Railroad.[8] On spur tracks, especially those in northern areas, coal-burning locomotives are still in operation. The Soviets also have huge stacks of assembled railway tracks ready for immediate use, also visible along the vital Trans-Siberian rail line.

If major cities were destroyed in nuclear strikes, railroad tracks would have to be laid around contaminated areas. This effort would be time-consuming but possible given the preparations already made by the Soviets for various emergencies.

Roads and Automotive Traffic

Control over road transport in a post-attack recovery period would be a simple matter: all transport would be under martial law. In time of peace a high percentage of the trucks used in Soviet civilian industries have mobilization designations. Since none of the trucks are privately owned in the first place, their use in recovery work would not be disputed. All other means of road transportation, from passenger automobiles to motorcycles, would also be placed under provisions of martial law and used as directed by the military command.

As noted previously, the Soviet Union does not have an extensive road system except in a few areas of European Russia. Neither is it dependent upon trucks for long-distance movement of freight, as is the United States. The number of automobiles owned by civilians, although increasing each year, is still relatively small.

For transportation near and around cities, trucks play a major role. Nuclear strikes would certainly damage parts of the many bypass roads that exist around major cities. This would slow restoration work, but trucks could still operate, since they are much simpler in design than those in the United States and can operate off paved surfaces. During dry summer months, or in the winter when the ground is frozen, trucks could operate cross-country. Spare parts for trucks could be produced in local blacksmith shops, as they often are at present. The limiting factor in truck transport following a nuclear strike probably would be fuel supplies.

Soviet aviation is well suited for such a task. *Aeroflot,* the Soviet airline, maintains many rugged, dependable, single-engine passenger aircraft capable of landing on sod fields or on ice and snow, and Soviet pilots are used to flying with simple navigational aids. Passengers and vital cargo should quickly reach outlying regions or those cut off from the rest of the nation.

Ties between the Ministry of Civil Aviation and the Soviet Air Forces are very close. At present there are two active-duty "chief marshals of aviation" in the Soviet Union. One heads the Soviet Air Forces; the other, Chief Marshal of Aviation B. P. Bugayev, serves as Minister of Civil Aviation and head of *Aeroflot.* In May 1970, Bugayev, then a general–colonel, was appointed to his present position, replacing Marshal of Aviation Ye. F. Loginov. In November 1973, Bugayev was promoted to Marshal of Aviation and in November 1977 to Chief Marshal of Aviation. Soviet air transport is militarized even in peacetime, and combining all aviation, civilian and military, under one control would not present any problems.

As in automotive transport, fuel supplies would likely be the most significant factor limiting air transport in a post-attack recovery operation.

Communications

Marshal Sokolovskiy's 1962 *Military Strategy* emphasized the need for duplicative communication facilities in preparation for a possible future war.[9] It is impossible to ascertain how communications might survive a nuclear strike and continue to function in the immediate post-strike period. Sophisticated electronic equipment would be severely damaged due to electromagnetic pulse (EMP) which would result from nuclear explosions. However, the Soviets are well aware of such a phenomenon, and may have hardened their communications equipment against this possibility. The continued widespread use of vacuum tubes, considered obsolete in the United States and other advanced technological societies, might even be an asset to the Soviets. Such tubes are less susceptible to EMP than are the advanced micro-circuits generally used in the United States.

The Communist Party maintains its own communications system throughout the U.S.S.R., as does the KGB. Military district headquarters operate lateral communication facilities, as well as direct lines to the Ministry of Defense and subordinate units. It should be anticipated that official Soviet communications could be restored rapidly following a nuclear strike.

Naturally, the ability of any nation to effect post-strike recovery would depend upon the level of the nuclear attack. If all warheads in the present U.S. strategic inventory were successfully delivered to targets in the Soviet Union, Soviet restoration efforts would likely prove impossible. If the attack was limited in scope, and if only selected targets were destroyed, the situation would be entirely different. In such an event, the greatest danger to Soviet recovery might well be the possibility of invasion by surrounding nations from which the Soviet Union has seized territory in the past.

NOTES

1. For a full discussion of SNAVR, see M. P. Tsivilev et al., *Inzhe-nerno-Spasatel'nyye i Neotlozhnyye Avariyno-Vosstanovitel'nyye Raboty v Ochage Yadernogo Porazheniya* [Engineer-Rescue and Urgent Disaster Restoration Work in Areas of Nuclear Destruction]. Moscow: Voyenizdat, 1975.

2. Leonid Brezhnev, *Rebirth,* published in Supplement V to *Socialism: Theory and Practice.* Moscow: Novosti Press Agency, 1978, p. 12.

3. Ibid., p. 18.

4. Ibid., p. 31.

5. Ibid., p. 35.

6. Ibid., p. 52.

7. Authors of this monograph have traveled the Trans-Siberian Railroad on five different occasions. The comments are based on personal observation.

8. During a 1972 rail trip, Moscow to Khabarovsk, the authors noted that their train, between Chita and Khabarovsk, was pulled by a World War II Lend-Lease locomotive. Such engines still can be seen, as of October-November 1979.

9. V. D. Sokolovskiy, *Soviet Military Strategy,* Third Edition, op. cit., pp. 328–329.

9
Conclusions

Capabilities

There is no certainty that any group governing a large, hetero-geneous population can design controls that would be effective throughout a nuclear war and in its aftermath. If such a system could be perfected, it probably exists in the Soviet Union. There are many statements in the Soviet press about how the Armed Forces, the national economy, and the population must be pre-pared for the eventuality of a nuclear war. This requirement is a basic tenet of Soviet military doctrine. One aspect of the Soviet approach is the constant indoctrination of the population in the belief that with preparation and training they can survive a nuclear exchange.

The Party–Government Control Structure

The control structure of the Soviet Union is many-faceted and overlapping. As noted earlier, its directing element is the Com-munist Party, which numbers approximately 17,430,000 out of a population of 265,000,000. Control is centralized in the Party's Central Committee's twenty-odd-member Politburo. This extreme centralization at the very top is duplicated in many respects at the union republic and lower levels of government. If the Politburo and its working Secretariat were destroyed by a nuclear strike or could not communicate with the remainder of the nation, the cen-tral committees and bureaus of the Party could continue to func-tion in the republics and at lower levels.

Decisions of the Party leaders are supported by the *Komsomol* (Young Communist League) members, who number approxi-mately 41,700,000. The *Komsomol* is a part of the Communist Party infrastructure. Support of the Party leadership also is pro-vided by the Professional Union of the U.S.S.R., with a mem-

bership of 128,000,000. Key individuals in both these organizations
are senior Party members, carefully selected.

The government structure in the Soviet Union provides the ve-
hicle by which the Communist Party leadership exercises its control over the nation. Key government positions actually are Party
positions and are held by trusted Party members. The government
structure, from the Supreme Soviet through the Council of Ministers, like that of the Party, is duplicated in its essential functions
in the union republics and *oblasts*. Even if major population centers were destroyed, some elements of the government would be
able to function.

Legal Measures

The Soviet Constitution provides for the declaration of martial
law when in the interests of the defense of the state, state security,
or maintenance of public order. Martial law would place the entire
nation, or specific areas, under control of the military council of
a front, army, or military district, or under command of troop
units in a given area. This law provides for the mobilization of all
labor and the issuance of edicts obligatory for the entire population. Nationwide martial law could be declared for the Soviet
Union in a period of tension.

There also are "wartime laws," defined as legal acts and regulations that are limited to a time of war. However, they might
be adopted by legislation before the nation enters a war, "but to
apply during the periods of the state of war." Wartime laws reg-
ulate civil, administrative, criminal, and other legal relationships,
and include the right to requisition goods and private property.

The legal system of the United States provides for the declaration of martial law, and on occasion regular military forces have
been called out to enforce government decisions. It would be difficult for Americans to visualize the enactment of martial law that
would extend throughout the United States. The Soviet people
have a different experience. Soviet leaders draw upon examples
from World War II to explain how martial law and wartime law
might be applied in the future. Major Soviet studies have been
made to reexamine the way in which interior regions supported

the military effort in the Great Patriotic War. To understand how the Soviet leadership might plan to maintain control in the event of a future war, it is necessary to study carefully how and what Soviet strategists in the 1970s and 1980s have written about the control structure that has served the Kremlin so well in the past.

Role of the Ministry of Defense

The relationship between the Party and the Ministry of Defense is a major element in the Soviet control structure. The higher military leadership rests in three bodies: the Council of Defense, the Main Military Council, and the General Staff.

The Council of Defense, made up essentially of key members of the Politburo, would be the directing body for the entire war effort, with its edicts having the force of law. Duplicate defense councils would be established at the republic level, comprised of key members of the bureaus of the union republics. The Main Military Council, now headed by the Minister of Defense, probably would be designated Headquarters of the Supreme High Command (the *Stavka* of the VGK), and also would be chaired by the Party's General Secretary. The General Staff would retain its current role, but with increased activity.

It should be expected that in a period of extreme tension the senior Party officials, including members of the Council of Ministers and top military leaders (many of whom are on the Central Committee), would leave Moscow for hardened shelters. They probably would be dispersed to different areas. Although a number could become victims of nuclear strikes, a sufficient cohort should survive to reestablish a centralized control body.

The General Staff, or its remaining elements following a nuclear exchange, would continue the function of military planning, coordinating the activities of all military forces including the various civil defense agencies. In those areas where martial law had been declared, the General Staff would be the link between defense councils and the military command in the area.

During the nuclear exchange as well as in the post-attack period, personnel of the five services — Strategic Rocket Forces, Ground Forces, Troops of Air Defense, Air Forces, and Navy — would provide disciplined forces. Support troops, such as Construction and Billeting, Rear Services, and Civil Defense, would be major assets to the military command and would provide a uniformed nucleus to work with civilian agencies. "Special troops," consisting of signal, engineer, chemical, road construction, automobile, and railroad troops, each with a chief who is responsible to the Minister of Defense, would be additional uniformed forces to assist the military commander.

Importance of Military Districts and Theaters of Military Operations

Theaters of military operations (TVDs) and the military districts within them would be most significant elements of the military structure in maintaining control during the attack phase In the post-attack period the TVD commander probably would be of less importance. Each of the sixteen military districts into which the entire Soviet Union is divided has elements of the Soviet Ground Forces, plus frontal aviation and Air Defense Troops.

In time of peace the military district headquarters are of sufficient size, with all necessary components, so that in time of war they could act as a TVD headquarters. If unable to communicate with its higher headquarters (which would be the *Stavka* of the VGK, through the General Staff in time of war), the TVD commander should be able to take independent military actions. This would be especially important if uprisings were to take place in an area that had been isolated from the remainder of the country by nuclear strikes.

The Party–military relationship at the military district level is of particular significance in terms of control. Under Soviet law, the local Party secretary serves on the military council of the military district. In turn, the military district commander and senior members of his staff generally serve on senior Party bodies, such as the bureaus of the Communist Party of the various republics. Thus, at the military district level, senior military figures also are senior Party figures. This joint Party–military structure would be an asset for maintaining control of the population during nuclear strikes, and for enforcing edicts concerning post-attack recovery. In effecting control, the military district commander would have the services of the military commissariat offices, which maintain records of all men and women subject to military service and of youths who have had training but have not yet been called up for active military duty. The list of all military reserve personnel in the area, maintained by the military commissariat office, also would be of great value to the local military authorities.

Role of the KGB and the MVD

Throughout the interior of the Soviet Union the KGB assists in control by means of informants and agents, who number in the millions. The head of the KGB is a senior general; KGB general officers are assigned to various duties in all the republics. In the event of nuclear strikes, KGB resources could supplement uniformed military forces under the local military commander. In border areas, where the elite KGB Border Guards operate, troops of the Ministry of Defense probably would be needed to help prevent an exodus should the Soviet Union come under nuclear attack.

The Minister of Internal Affairs, like the head of the KGB, is a senior general. Detachments of Internal Troops, based in or near all major Soviet cities, would be in position to take immediate action during a nuclear war. The local militia, also under MVD control, are lightly armed. In the panic that would result from nuclear strikes, they probably would require the immediate support of Internal Troops. Some help could be given by the "People's Guard," currently consisting of several million volunteers.

Soviet firemen, also under the MVD, are a militarized force with military ranks. They could work closely with civil defense in any emergency, a task for which they are trained during peacetime.

Whatever the emergency or situation, even nuclear attack, the Soviet leadership visualizes the Party retaining its dominant role. Actions of all control bodies, such as military commanders, KGB personnel, and Internal Troop units, would be in the name of the Party.

Civil Defense

The Soviet civil defense program is the most visible evidence of the Kremlin's planning for population survival in the event of a nuclear war. Those individuals assigned to civil defense duties, both military and civilian, provide a trained cadre who, through current programs, helps prepare the population psychologically for the possibility of a nuclear attack and gives instructions on evacuation measures and shelter construction. Should nuclear strikes occur, all inhabitants in the area would be engaged in civil defense work.

Assignment of civil defense responsibilities to a four-star general, who also is a Deputy Minister of Defense, provides means and authority to accomplish this task. Troops of civil defense, under control of military district commanders, are located in or adjacent to large cities. The deputy chief for civil defense in the military district headquarters can work directly with the chief of staff for civil defense (who also is a general officer) in each of the republics.

The effectiveness of the Soviet civil defense program is a much debated topic in the United States. Certain facts about the program are irrefutable: the chief of civil defense is a Deputy Minister of Defense; general officers are assigned to military district headquarters for civil defense matters; there are Troops of Civil Defense; Soviet general officers who can be identified by name serve as chiefs of staff for civil defense in the union republics; officers of other military ranks serve in similar capacities at lower administrative levels; there are civil defense training requirements for the populace as a whole. A civil defense infrastructure exists in reality.

With respect to controlling the population in the event of a nuclear war, the Soviet civil defense capability must be analyzed in conjunction with the total Soviet power structure. Party organizations, the state control mechanism, forces of the Ministry of Defense, and KGB and MVD resources would be in full support of, and a part of Soviet civil defense, should the Soviet Union come under nuclear attack.

Vulnerabilities

There is no reasonable method to determine the effectiveness, or vulnerabilities, of the Soviet control structure. The Soviet system of economics, education, construction, etc., do not perform as the Party intends, nor as Soviet spokesmen claim. Goals of five-year plans seldom are met; housing throughout the Soviet Union, almost forty years following the end of World War II, remains substandard. Foodstuffs must be imported from abroad. The same indifference, corruption, mismanagement, and other problems epidemic to the Soviet state must also apply, in one way or another, to the ability of the Soviet leadership to maintain control in event of a nuclear war.

Would the Soviet leadership in the initial period of a nuclear war be able to operate more efficiently than did their predecessors in 1941? The Soviet people have never been told that on June 22, 1941, when Hitler launched his invasion, Stalin completely lost control of himself. It was not until July 3 that he gained enough self-control to make his first wartime radio address. Nor are the Soviet people told that during the first weeks of the attack the population of hundreds of villages welcomed the Germans as liberators. Millions of Soviet citizens died during the "Great Patriotic War" as the result of mistakes made by Stalin and his staff. The thousands of articles and books published each year about the "Great Patriotic War" are idealized accounts of what actually happened.

Even in the 1980s, force is required to keep the many Soviet nationality groups in line. Native elements in the Baltic republics still are hostile to Soviet rule. Demographic changes in the Soviet population show a continuing decrease in the percentage of Soviet people who are Slavs. If the internal control structure will be strained as a result of nuclear strikes, while at the same time the Soviet Armed Forces are engaged in an offensive against NATO forces, chaos throughout the Soviet Union may result. Uprisings might occur in any number of minority groups, from the Estonians, Ukrainians, Georgians, and Moldavians to the Moslem nationalities around the Black Sea, the Caspian Sea, and in Central Asia. Some of these groups might want simply to break away from the U.S.S.R., others would strive for a different kind of socialist political system, while others might want to be reunited with groups outside the Soviet borders.

A major danger to the Soviet Union in the wake of nuclear strikes would be its neighbors. The Soviet Union has no real allies except possibly Bulgaria. If Soviet military forces and the control structure were seriously weakened, would its neighbors remain passive? Major Soviet forces are deployed opposite China. However, the vast areas of the U.S.S.R. east of the Ural Mountains and the Caspian Sea are linked only by a few key rail lines and air routes. If rail lines were damaged, the great distances involved in the region would make it extremely difficult to move sufficient materials to supply a modern military force. With resupply uncertain from Western Soviet areas, forces along the long Chinese border would be in a difficult position, should the Chinese choose to attack.

The nations of Eastern Europe probably would quickly seek to throw off Soviet rule should the Soviet Union be weakened significantly by nuclear strikes. Should the Chinese attack in the East, then nations such as Rumania and Poland might seek to regain territory that previously had been taken from them by the Soviet Union.

Unless all the nations along the Soviet borders, from Finland to China, were also to experience nuclear strikes, many likely would turn on a partially destroyed Soviet Union. Were Soviet forces in the interior of the nation required to concentrate on fighting foreign invaders rather than on maintaining internal control, the Soviet structure could collapse. Successful uprisings by the many nationality groups could take place, and post-attack recovery within areas still supporting a communist regime might be impossible or delayed.

The severe climate in the greater part of the Soviet Union limits not only the food that can be produced for the population, but also would lessen chances for survival of the population that might be driven out of cities undergoing nuclear attack. As demonstrated during World War II, the ability of the Soviet people to survive under most difficult conditions should not be discounted. Nevertheless, lack of food combined with cold and damaged transportation lines would seriously hinder the Kremlin's ability to wage a protracted war, or to effect post-attack recovery.

If the Soviet Union were in no danger from its neighbors following a nuclear strike, it is possible that the Party–military combination could maintain control and effect recovery. But if the Soviet Union were forced to send its military forces to its borders to counter a Chinese attack, face a massive uprising among its Eastern European satellites, and be prepared for an attack from the nations of Western Europe, could the nation survive?

The Soviet leadership may be in a quandary. They have no dependable allies. If the nation were damaged significantly in a nuclear exchange with the United States, and if other nuclear powers — China, Britain, and France — were untouched, Soviet forces would have to remain on alert for the possibility of strikes from these remaining nuclear powers. Soviet conventional forces would be required along the borders to prevent possible invasions from its neighbors. This could leave insufficient forces in the interior of the nation to control minority groups and dissidents. The Party leadership might be faced with the choice of maintaining internal control or sending forces to defend Soviet borders. This would not be an easy decision.

Western strategic planners must recognize that the Soviet command and control structure is greatly different from that of the United States, or any other NATO nation. How well would this Soviet structure withstand a protracted war, either conventional or nuclear, or a combination of the two? Would nuclear strikes on this same structure bring a rapid end to nuclear exchanges? Or should nuclear targeting be counterforce — to attack, in the event of war, only the Soviet Armed Forces?

The primary military task of the United States and its allies is to maintain sufficient strength to deter the Soviet Union from creating a situation that would lead to war. A deterrent force is effective only if it has a true warfighting capability. An understanding of the Soviet command and control structure is essential in deciding what forces are necessary to deter the Kremlin, and to repulse Soviet military aggression if required. It is hoped that this analysis will contribute to this understanding.

APPENDIX

Divisions of Management in the Council of Ministers

As noted in Chapter 3, the primary function of the Supreme Soviet is to "elect" the Council of Ministers, the actual management body of the Soviet government. The Council of Ministers consists of the following:

- *Chairman*
- *First Vice Chairman*
- *Thirteen Vice Chairmen*
- *Thirty-three All-Union Ministries:* Automotive Industry; Aviation Industry; Chemical Industry; Chemical and Petroleum Machine Building; Civil Aviation; Communication Equipment Industry; Construction of Petroleum and Gas Industry Enterprises; Construction, Road and Municipal Machine Building; Defense; Defense Industry; Electrical Equipment Industry; Electronics Industry; Fertilizer Production; Foreign Trade; Far East and Trans-Baikal Construction; Gas Industry; General Machine Building; Heavy and Transport Machine Building; Instrument Making, Automation Equipment and Control Systems; Machine Building; Machine Building for Animal Husbandry and Fodder Production; Machine Building for Light and Food Industries and Domestic Devices; Machine Tool and Instrument Industry; Maritime Fleet; Medical Industry; Medium Machine Building; Petroleum Industry; Power Machine Building; Radio Industry; Railways; Shipbuilding Industry; Tractor and Agricultural Machine Building; Transport Construction.
- *Thirty-one Union Republic Ministries:* Agriculture; Coal Industry; Communications; Construction of Heavy Industry Enterprises; Construction Materials Industry; Culture; Education; Ferrous Metallurgy; Finance; Fish Industry; Food Industry; Foreign Affairs; Fruit and Vegetable Culture; Geology; Health; Higher and Secondary Specialized Education; Industrial Construction; Installation and Special Construction Work; Internal Affairs; Justice; Land Reclamation and Water Resources; Light Industry; Meat and Dairy In-

dustry; Nonferrous Metallurgy; Petroleum Refining and Petrochemical Industry; Power and Electrification; Procurement; Rural Construction; Timber, Pulp, Paper and Wood Processing Industry; Trade; Construction.

- *Six All-Union State Committees:* Foreign Economic Relations; Hydrometeorology and Control of Natural Resources; Inventions and Discoveries; Material Reserves; Science and Technology; Standards.
- *Twelve Union Republic State Committees:* Agricultural Technical Support Production; Cinematography; Construction Affairs; Forestry; Labor and Social Problems; Material and Technical Supply; Petroleum Products Supply; Planning (GOSPLAN); Prices; Publishing Houses, Printing Plants and the Book Trade; State Security; Television and Radio Broadcasting; Vocational and Technical Education.
- *Three "Other Agencies":* for General Affairs of the Council of Ministers; Board of the State Bank; Central Statistical Administration. Also the Committee of People's Control.[1]

1. The composition of the Council of Ministers, U.S.S.R., frequently changes. Listings given here come from the *Yezhegodnik* of the *Bol'shaya Sovetskaya Entsiklopediya,* 1981, pp. 13–14.

National Strategy Information Center, Inc.

PUBLICATIONS

Gerald L. Steibel, Editor
Joyce E. Larson, Associate Editor
William C. Bodie, Associate Editor

BOOKS

Arms, Men, and Military Budgets: Issues for Fiscal Year 1981 by Francis P. Hoeber, William Schneider, Jr., Norman Polmar, and Ray Bessette, May 1980

Arms, Men, and Military Budgets: Issues for Fiscal Year 1979, by Francis P. Hoeber, David B. Kassing, and William Schneider, Jr., February 1978

Arms, Men, and Military Budgets: Issues for Fiscal Year 1978, edited by Francis P. Hoeber and William Schneider, Jr., May 1977

Arms, Men, and Military Budgets: Issues for Fiscal Year 1977, edited by William Schneider, Jr., and Francis P. Hoeber, May 1976

* * *

Intelligence Requirements for the 1980s: Clandestine Collection (Volume V of a Series) edited by Roy Godson, November 1982

Intelligence Requirements for the 1980s: Covert Action (Volume IV of a Series) edited by Roy Godson, September 1981

Intelligence Requirements for the 1980s: Counterintelligence (Volume III of a Series) edited by Roy Godson, January 1981

Intelligence Requirements for the 1980s: Analysis and Estimates (Volume II of a Series) edited by Roy Godson, June 1980

Intelligence Requirements for the 1980s: Elements of Intelligence (Volume I of a Series) edited by Roy Godson, October 1979

* * *

The Soviet View of U.S. Strategic Doctrine by Jonathan Samuel Lockwood, April 1983

Strategic Military Suprise: Incentives and Opportunities edited by Klaus Knorr and Patrick Morgan, January 1983

National Security Affairs: Theoretical Perspectives and Contemporary Issues edited by B. Thomas Trout and James E. Harf, October 1982

False Science: Underestimating the Soviet Arms Buildup by Steven Rosefielde, July 1982

Our Changing Geopolitical Premises by Thomas P. Rona, January 1982

Strategic Minerals: A Resource Crisis published by the Council on Economics and National Security (an NSIC Project), December 1981

U.S. Policy and Low-Intensity Conflict: Potentials for Military Struggles in the 1980s edited by Sam C. Sarkesian and William L. Scully, June 1981

New Foundations for Asian and Pacific Security edited by Joyce E. Larson, September 1980

The Fateful Ends and Shades of SALT: Past . . . Present . . . And Yet to Come? by Paul H. Nitze, James E. Dougherty, and Francis X. Kane, March 1979

Strategic Options for the Early Eighties: What Can Be Done? edited by William R. Van Cleave and W. Scott Thompson, February 1979

Oil, Divestiture and National Security edited by Frank N. Trager, December 1976 (Out of print)

Indian Ocean Naval Limitations, Regional Issues and Global Implications by Alvin J. Cottrell and Walter F. Hahn, April 1976

* * *

The Intelligent Layperson's Guide to the Nuclear Freeze and Peace Debate by Joyce E. Larson and William C. Bodie, March 1983

War and Peace: Soviet Russia Speaks edited by Albert L. Weeks and William C. Bodie, with an essay by Frank R. Barnett, March 1983

STRATEGY PAPERS

The Soviet Control Structure: Capabilities for Wartime Survival by Harriet Fast Scott and William F. Scott, August 1983

Strategic Weapons: An Introduction by Norman Polmar, October 1975. Revised edition, June 1982

Conventional War and Escalation: The Soviet View by Joseph D. Douglass, Jr. and Amoretta M. Hoeber, November 1981

Soviet Perceptions of Military Doctrine and Military Power: The Interaction of Theory and Practice by John J. Dziak, June 1981

How Little is Enough? SALT and Security in the Long Run by Francis P. Hoeber, January 1981

Raw Material Supply in a Multipolar World by Yuan-li Wu, October 1973. Revised edition, October 1979

India: Emergent Power? by Stephen P. Cohen and Richard L. Park, June 1978

The Kremlin and Labor: A Study in National Security Policy by Roy Godson, November 1977

The Evolution of Soviet Security Strategy 1965-1975 by Avigdor Haselkorn, November 1977

The Geopolitics of the Nuclear Era by Colin S. Gray, September 1977

The Sino-Soviet Confrontation: Implications for the Future by Harold C. Hinton, September 1976 (Out of print)

Food, Foreign Policy, and Raw Materials Cartels by William Schneider, Jr., February 1976

Soviet Sources of Military Doctrine and Strategy by William F. Scott, July 1975

Detente: Promises and Pitfalls by Gerald L. Steibel, March 1975 (Out of print)

Oil, Politics and Sea Power: The Indian Ocean Vortex by Ian W. A. C. Adie, December 1974 (Out of print)

The Soviet Presence in Latin America by James D. Theberge, June 1974

The Horn of Africa by J. Bowyer Bell, Jr., December 1973

Research and Development and the Prospects for International Security by Frederick Seitz and Rodney W. Nichols, December 1973

The People's Liberation Army: Communist China's Armed Forces by Angus M. Fraser, August 1973 (Out of print)

Nuclear Weapons and the Atlantic Alliance by Wynfred Joshua, May 1973 (Out of print)

How to Think About Arms Control and Disarmament by James E. Dougherty, May 1973 (Out of print)

The Military Indoctrination of Soviet Youth by Leon Goure, January 1973 (Out of print)

The Asian Alliance: Japan and United States Policy by Franz Michael and Gatson J. Sigur, October 1972 (Out of print)

Iran, the Arabian Peninsula, and the Indian Ocean by R. M. Burrell and Alvin J. Cottrell, September 1972 (Out of print)

Soviet Naval Power: Challenge for the 1970s by Norman Polmar, April 1972. Revised edition, September 1974 (Out of print)

How Can We Negotiate with the Communists? by Gerald L. Steibel, March 1972 (Out of print)

Soviet Political Warfare Techniques, Espionage and Propaganda in the 1970s by Lyman B. Kirkpatrick, Jr., and Howland H. Sargeant, January 1972 (Out of print)

The Soviet Presence in the Eastern Mediterranean by Lawrence L. Whetten, September 1971 (Out of print)

The Military Unbalance: Is the U.S. Becoming a Second Class Power? June 1971 (Out of print)

The Future of South Vietnam by Brigadier F. P. Serong, February 1971 (Out of print)

Strategy and National Interests: Reflections for the Future by Bernard Brodie, January 1971 (Out of print)

145

The Mekong River: A Challenge in Peaceful Development for Southeast Asia by Eugene R. Black, December 1970 (Out of print)

Problems of Strategy in the Pacific and Indian Oceans by George C. Thomson, October 1970 (Out of print)

Soviet Penetration into the Middle East by Wynfred Joshua, July 1970. Revised edition, October 1971 (Out of print)

Australian Security Policies and Problems by Justus M. Van der Kroef, May 1970 (Out of print)

Detente: Dilemma or Disaster? by Gerald L. Steibel, July 1969 (Out of print)

The Prudent Case for Safeguard by William R. Kintner, June 1969 (Out of print)

AGENDA PAPERS

The China Sea: The American Stake in its Future by Harold C. Hinton, January 1981

NATO, Turkey, and the Southern Flank: A Midwestern Perspective by Ihsan Gurkan, March 1980

The Soviet Threat to NATO's Northern Flank by Marian K. Leighton, November 1979

Does Defense Beggar Welfare? Myths Versus Realities by James L. Clayton, June 1979 (Out of print)

Naval Race or Arms Control in the Indian Ocean? (Some Problems in Negotiating Naval Limitations) by Alvin Cottrell and Walter F. Hahn, September 1978 (Out of print)

Power Projection: A Net Assessment of U.S. and Soviet Capabilities by W. Scott Thompson, April 1978

Understanding the Soviet Military Threat, How CIA Estimates Went Astray by William T. Lee, February 1977 (Out of print)

Toward a New Defense for NATO, The Case for Tactical Nuclear Weapons, July 1976 (Out of print)

Seven Tracks to Peace in the Middle East by Frank R. Barnett, April 1975

Arms Treaties with Moscow: Unequal Terms Unevenly Applied? by Donald G. Brennan, April 1975 (Out of print)

Toward a U.S. Energy Policy by Klaus Knorr, March 1975 (Out of print)

Can We Avert Economic Warfare in Raw Materials? US Agriculture as a Blue Ship by William Schneider, Jr., July 1974

The National Strategy Information Center is a nonpartisan tax-exempt institution organized in 1962 to conduct educational programs in national defense.

The Center espouses no political causes. Its Directors and Officers represent a wide spectrum of responsible political opinion from liberal to conservative. What unites them, however, is the conviction that neither isolationism nor pacificism provides realistic solutions to the challenge of 20th century totalitarianism.

NSIC exists to encourage civil-military partnership on the grounds that, in a democracy, informed public opinion is necessary to a viable U.S defense system capable of protecting the nation's vital interests and assisting other free nations which aspire to independence and self-fulfillment.